Never
Let Go

For Family A:
Jack who saved me. Issy who found me.
Ross who saw me.

Never Let Go

How to Parent Your Child Through Mental Illness

Suzanne Alderson

Vermilion
LONDON

Published in 2020 by Vermilion, an imprint of Ebury Publishing,
20 Vauxhall Bridge Road,
London SW1V 2SA

Vermilion is part of the Penguin Random House group of companies
whose addresses can be found at global.penguinrandomhouse.com

Penguin
Random House
UK

First published in the United Kingdom by Vermilion in 2020

www.penguin.co.uk

A CIP catalogue record for this book is available from the British Library

ISBN 9781785043314

Printed and bound in Great Britain by Clays Ltd, Elcograf S.p.A.

The authorised representative in the EEA is Penguin Random House
Ireland, Morrison Chambers, 32 Nassau Street, Dublin D02 YH68

Penguin Random House is committed to a
sustainable future for our business, our readers
and our planet. This book is made from Forest
Stewardship Council® certified paper.

The information in this book has been compiled by way of general guidance
in relation to the specific subjects addressed. It is not a substitute and not to
be relied on for medical, healthcare, pharmaceutical or other professional
advice on specific circumstances and in specific locations. Please consult
your GP before changing, stopping or starting any medical treatment. So
far as the author is aware the information given is correct and up to date as
at August 2020. All names in cases studies have been changed. Practice,
laws and regulations all change, and the reader should obtain up to date
professional advice on any such issues. The author and publishers disclaim,
as far as the law allows, any liability arising directly or indirectly from the
use, or misuse, of the information contained in this book.

Contents

Introduction

If you're a parent of a child suffering with poor mental health and you've picked up this book, you're probably seeking answers to questions you never considered you'd need to ask. Let's be honest, it's not a typical parental hope for our child to suffer mental distress, is it? We don't dream of seeing our child medicated, or self-harming, or fighting an illness that hinders their ability to engage with the world.

Mental illness challenges every belief and fact we think we know about parenting. It inverts the rules and changes the game. It floods us with self-doubt and separates us from the life we were living before it turned up. From my experiences with mental illness, I can say that the act of caring for someone with a mental disorder is a truly unique one; life-changing, life-challenging and life-affirming, if you allow it to be.

When mental illness happens, which it increasingly does to many of our young people, we find ourselves woefully ill-equipped to deal with the shock and fear we face. We may also have to deal with the everyday, practical implications, the judgements of society and our own misplaced self-flagellation for 'letting this happen'. The world we now face is frightening and isolating, fuelled by fear and magnified by shame. Everything we knew is no longer certain. Everything we hoped for is no longer likely. We can't rely on the truths we believed, and we're simply not prepared for the extreme experiences, emotions and never-ending questions that are sprung upon us by this hateful illness.

Some of the questions shouting for attention will be around your child's current state: What on earth is going on? What do I do now? How do we cope? Is this forever? How can I fix this? Others will be about their future and the uncertainty that now colours every thought about your family: Will they ever recover or live independently? What does this mean for their future? Do they even have one? The hardest questions to answer may be those you ask yourself in the quiet of the night: Did I make this happen? Why didn't I stop it? What kind of two-bit parent am I?

This is *almost* the book I wanted to read when I was supporting my daughter through her mental illness. I say that because I could spend my life writing about this experience and all I've learned, and it would never be complete. I set out to write this book because I wanted to download and impart all the learnings and experiences from the past five years of caring for my daughter through her chronic mental illness. I wanted to share the experiences of parents in the Parenting Mental Health community (see page 3), something I started to support, connect and also educate other parents.

In the middle of the night, some months after my daughter's mental health crisis began, I found myself sitting in her bedroom as she slept, listening to her breathe, needing to be sure she was still alive. I was trying to untangle the same jumble of questions you may be facing and to come to terms with the enormous pain that I carried everywhere and couldn't put down. I was suddenly struck by the notion that I couldn't be the only parent going through this; we couldn't be the only family in this situation. It just wasn't possible. And in that moment of connection, with persons unknown, some of the pain I felt was transformed into an urgent and powerful drive and desire to connect with others and to help them through.

And so I set up a Facebook group (see page 3) to give other parents the kind of support and information I couldn't find and to help them understand the unique and powerful role they have in their child's mental illness. Over the past few years, we've helped, supported and connected over 20,000 parents through our digital platforms, and we are now a charity with a mission to end generational mental illness.

My intention with this book is to extend a hand to you as you travel this path and share the highs and lows as you make sense of a nonsensical time. I hope this is the beginning of a conversation. Between you and me. Between you and the people around you. Between you and your child and your family. And between you and yourself. In time, I hope our conversations lead to another with society, because this problem isn't going away and we need to make changes now, not just as individuals, but as a collective.

> Throughout the book I have included case studies from members of the Parenting Mental Health community who have kindly shared their experiences. If you'd like to read more, please join us in the private community on Facebook. Search for 'Parenting Mental Health', and you'll find a link to join the group at the top of the page. Please answer the three questions when you request to join. It's essential that the community remains a safe haven and a closed space, solely for those who are experiencing the challenge and distress of their child's mental health illness.

As you navigate this new path – one you don't want to tread, one without a map, one where the destination is unclear and may not even exist – I want this book and the community behind it to be your companion, in every sense of the word.

Like a trusted friend, we are here for you – for you to rely on and remind you that you're not alone. I want this book to give you the comfort you need when you're faced with the uncertainty of mental illness, as well as the confidence to challenge and stamp your feet and get the professional support your child needs. I want you to scribble in it and underline it and highlight it and make it something you'll reflect on over time, to see how far you've come and what has changed.

Most of all, I want to give you hope. That you can get through this together; that you will be stronger because of the experience; that things won't be the same and that's OK. They can even end up being better. Recovery is a practice, not a destination.

My hope is that, in time, you'll be where I am now; looking back at a chaotic storm that flattened the world as we knew it, and living a different future that we'd never considered, built to fit us. While there were times I could not conceive of my daughter surviving, let alone thriving, I am delighted to say that she did both. Issy is now living a happy, purposeful life on her terms, having recovered fully from mental illness.

Once you understand the power of the storm, of your power to get through it and the changes it has enforced, I hope you'll extend your hand to someone else who is just starting to experience what you have come through.

I understand this is the rockiest, most challenging path you'll likely have found yourself on as a parent, and you have no idea if you'll make it through or what shape you'll be in at the end. I know that you *can* make it through and I hope that my experiences can help you do just that.

The simple act of being here, reading this book, is at once a tiny step and a huge leap in coming to terms with the fact that life has changed and you and your child are now at war. But not with each other. You're at war with mental illness.

And while I know you really don't want to be here, and I know you probably wonder how on earth I could understand your pain, I do. I'm with you all the way.

Suzanne

How to use this book

Whatever stage you are at in your child's mental illness, I hope you will see this book as your companion to the challenges, changes and emotions you face as you support your child through – a trusted guide that will give you support and information as you navigate the practical and emotional challenges of this experience.

Start at the beginning and read it in order, or dip in to the chapters that call to you. Write notes in it, highlight sections and use it as your personal reference throughout this experience.

I'd love to welcome you to the Parenting Mental Health community (see page 3 for details of how to join) and to start a conversation, email: info@ parentingmentalhealth.com.

1

Issy's Story

I need to start this book by telling you Issy's story. This is my account of what led to her becoming mentally ill, how we felt as parents and how we supported Issy to recover. I will share how we changed and came through this as a stronger family, and I will show you that there is hope.

I knew our lives had changed on Monday, 12 October 2015. The morning began just like every other had for the past few weeks. I carried a vague feeling of unease that something was happening and I wasn't sure I wanted to believe it or conceive of its potential for damage. Just as I had every other day for months, I was hiding, and hoping that my love and concern would overcome what was threatening to consume our daughter. But that day *wasn't* like any other and, by the end of it, our lives would be unrecognisable. I would no longer be able to hide and there would be no way I could avoid facing what was happening in our home.

Our 14-year-old daughter, Issy, had been bullied for at least a year and it was having an increasing impact on her mental health. She had stopped eating, she wasn't sleeping and getting her out of the house was becoming impossible. I wasn't sure at the time if these behaviours were by-products of the bullying that would ease and disappear if things at school improved. I do know that I wasn't prepared to have a depressed, anxious daughter; I simply couldn't believe that was the case and that I hadn't prevented it. Until that memorable day, my brain blocked out all thoughts of clinical mental illness and I genuinely hoped things would improve with time and our love.

Before that day, Issy had been struggling to get to school and we'd spent many hours sitting in the school car park or with the nurse. If she made it in to school, she would come out pale, exhausted and so desperately, deeply sorry for something she had no control over. We would end each day with the same resolve to try again tomorrow. The nurse suggested that Issy needed professional help, as all the low-level techniques to get her in to class had failed. She referred her to CAMHS – the Children and Adolescent Mental Health Services – and informed us the wait would be at least nine weeks. I was horrified. How were we supposed to cope in the meantime? Our daughter was fading away before our eyes, in every sense. The nurse suggested we visit our doctor to see if he could speed up the referral process. After our initial consultation, the GP offered Issy a series of further appointments to keep her going until the CAMHS appointment came through.

So here we were, walking to the doctor's room for the first of these interim appointments. Suddenly, Issy asked if she could go in and see the doctor alone. I was a little surprised, as we were very close, but naturally I agreed. I told the GP I'd be outside when they finished. My mind was in a whirl as I sat waiting; half wondering whether he could help, half wondering what we needed help for. When Issy finally emerged with the doctor, he told us to head home and that he would call me. The conversation during the car journey home didn't extend to what they'd discussed, so when I picked up the phone to the doctor half an hour later I was in no way prepared for what he told me. His words changed our lives forever.

The doctor told me that my perfect girl intended to end her own life, that she had a plan to do it and that she was going to act on it imminently. And our lives changed in that moment.

After the bombshell

The GP told me to not leave her alone and that he would refer her urgently to CAMHS. I don't remember much more of the conversation as I was in shock at what he had told me and I just wanted to get off the phone to go to Issy. I needed to see her, to let her know that she wasn't alone, that I was there for her and that, even though I had no idea how, we would get through this.

When I went into her room, she was deeply upset and apologetic for what the doctor had had to tell me: sorry that she felt that way, sorry that she hadn't been able to tell me, sorry that she wasn't able to stop the feelings. She had tried so, so hard.

We hugged and cried as I told her that she didn't have anything to apologise for, it was OK, and that I would do anything and everything to help her. But the truth was I didn't know how to. All I knew was that I intended to ensure she got through this – whatever 'this' was, however long it would last and whatever it might become.

I texted my husband and asked him to go somewhere private and call me. Saying the words out loud that your beautiful child intends to end her life is a gut-wrenching and surreal experience. Saying them to the other person in the world who loves her as much as you do is highly distressing. I struggled to explain what had happened with the doctor and, as I tried to make sense of my own emotions, I wasn't explicit enough for him to grasp the enormity of the situation. It was as if my head wouldn't allow my mouth to say what had just happened. Perhaps if I didn't say it out loud then it wouldn't be true? After skirting around the subject, much to my husband's frustration, I eventually used the only word that reflected the severity and reality of the situation: 'suicide'. And at this point, we both broke down.

My husband came home immediately, desperate to see what we could do to help our daughter and needing to check for himself that she was safe. Sitting with this unbelievable reality, we were stunned and somewhat incredulous that we – us, our family – could be in this situation. We were both wrestling with the same questions: How did we get here? How had it got this bad? How did we allow this to happen? And how on earth are we going to get through it?

The rest of the day was a blur. We sat with our daughter and tried to begin to make sense of a completely senseless situation. She was overwhelmed that it was out in the open and spent much of the rest of the day asleep, with me sitting by, watching her breathe. After a sleepless night, the doctor called with an appointment for her to see a psychiatrist at CAMHS the next day. And so it began, the most challenging, transformative time of our lives.

How did we get here?

One question I asked myself over and over again was, 'How did this happen?' I knew the facts of *why* we were in this position, but I couldn't fathom *how* we'd allowed ourselves to get here. We are a loving and connected family and, as parents, our decisions and choices have prioritised our children since our son arrived 26 years ago. Issy was always very much like my husband: creative, smart and incredibly funny. As a young child, she brought an endearing mix of humour and sassiness to everything she touched. She was kind and loving, happy and quirky. A creator, she loved making things, drawing and baking, and was generally at her happiest outside exploring nature.

> *'I thought I had depression when I was 13, when I found out what it was. It became so normal to me to feel that way, it hadn't just happened, and it felt like this was just what I was like so I didn't think I needed help. Until it got worse.'*
>
> Issy

If I reflect on life before Issy became ill, I would have to say that she was always a little different from most children. She thought differently and saw the world differently, and this was something we always embraced and encouraged. But uniqueness is a curse for a child if she can't find someone who sees the same magic and can fight against the norm alongside her. And when we moved her to a different school at the age of nine, we unwittingly placed her somewhere that didn't appreciate her quirks as we did, and wasn't interested in the curiosity and sense of wonder that enabled her to explore the world around her in her unique way. Reports from her new school told us she was conscientious and quiet, but, as the next couple of years passed, we slowly and silently lost sight of the effervescent child we knew and loved.

About a year before her disclosure to the doctor, Issy began to dread school and anxiety set in. It started gradually, until she would cry in the car before or after school four days out of five. She stopped going out with friends. She was in a constant state of heightened fear; a tiny twig on the ground became a spider (a phobia of hers at the time) and she jumped at the slightest sound. If someone tried to engage her in conversation she would go pale and look to me for support. We made excuses for her not to attend family events and shielded her from as much as we could, including allowing her to stay off ill from school with every kind of ache that masked the fact her mind was in overdrive. Looking back, I can see that she had reached her capacity to cope, yet I still wasn't ready or able to acknowledge what was going on.

I used a mix of ways to support Issy during this time. I started to take the pressure off and simplified her life as much as I could, not putting her in situations that would expose her to anxiety. I took her for regular hypnotherapy. I tried to be the best friend I could to her as her mother. Dealing with the bullies became the highest priority for me and my husband, but, for Issy, it created more anxiety. My husband spoke to the school and they agreed to move the two bullies to another class for the coming term. As we drove to school on the first day back after the break, Issy told me she'd got this; she was nervous but believed the change would help. But later that day, a distressing call from her told me that the school hadn't remembered to move the bullies and they were in her class and sitting by her.

We quickly spoke to the school and appeared to have resolved the issue, but by the end of the second week of term, Issy had been off more than she had attended. She was struggling with stomach aches, headaches, heartaches – every type of ache imaginable; anything not to go to school. I was still keeping up the pretence that this was under control – something that love, a hug and a slab of Victoria sponge could fix. I knew that the pain she was fighting stemmed from the situation at school, but I didn't comprehend what the implications of that would be for her. I didn't recognise that her mental health was in sharp decline. It wasn't that I didn't want to help; quite the opposite. I didn't *hear* what her actions were telling me. I couldn't confront the fact that what I thought was supportive parenting wasn't working; being a parent was something I'd always found rewarding and natural. This was out of my hands and escaping me, and I had no idea how to deal with it. Issy was retreating from life and yet, still, we didn't see it as something that needed professional intervention.

Why didn't we see it?

I have spent many hours since that day Issy spoke to the GP cross-examining myself on why I blocked out the possibility that Issy had a mental health issue. It was certainly not through any kind of wilful neglect. I have reasoned it was more overly optimistic ignorance and holding on to the future. Sometimes as a parent, you're so intent on the future, you don't spend enough time in the present. So, contemplating that Issy may have been mentally ill only came to my attention when I'd tried all the tools in my kit and her actions showed that she couldn't continue.

I didn't know how to explain to people why she couldn't go to school. No one seemed to understand how serious things were becoming, how intangible and hard to define the situation was, how unwieldy it all felt or what we should do next. Up to this point, there was a sense that if I didn't acknowledge mental illness and marked the changes we were seeing up to being bullied or being a teenager, or added in more tactical support as a parent, then it wouldn't get worse and I could still manage it. How wrong and naive I was. I had believed that if I loved hard enough and supported well enough, with sprinklings of help from a therapist, some time off or a calming meditation track, I could nudge Issy and us back on to the track of the life we'd been living before she was bullied. At no point did I consider she had a clinical mental illness.

Mental illness isn't like chickenpox. You don't suddenly wake up one day and you're covered with the mental equivalent of spots and realise you have a mental health disorder. It slips into your life slowly and silently and you can't always join the dots of what has gone on until you look back.

Changing our approach

Unfortunately, Issy's revelation to our doctor that she had a plan to end her life wasn't the end of it. She was suicidal for quite some time, attempted to end her life and continued to be seriously ill for far longer than we expected. It was the start of many, many challenging months. Days spent wondering when we would wake from this nightmare; hours in the psychiatrist's office; in therapy appointments; or in car parks drinking tea at midnight to stop her harming herself. Too many moments spent trying to shut up the mind monkeys that told me with a mix of disdain and delight that I was a failure of a mother and I'd caused this. And a constant energy focused on fighting the world, the framework of society, the norms, the expectations, while trying to contain the deep fear that we'd lose her.

Some days, it felt that, unlike a physical illness, the drive for recovery was solely so Issy could return to her place on the conveyor belt of life, whether that was right for her, or helpful, or whether she was fully healed or not. The clinical focus was on moving her out of a state of crisis as quickly as possible, but this didn't take into account why she had become suicidal or explore what she needed to live a balanced and happy life going forward. It seemed that if she wasn't a threat to herself, that was enough justification to place her back into the structures that had led her to want to end her life. But we learned the hard way that that approach doesn't work.

I spoke to my husband about when he knew we needed a new approach and he immediately said it was when we were sitting in A&E with Issy. He knew we had to change the way we managed her illness, because her mental health was declining fast and we were losing her. For me, it had been a gradual realisation. Her actions and responses were shouting at us that she couldn't and wouldn't go back to the life she had lived before and, if we didn't listen to her, we would lose her. Forcing her to conform to general expectations about recovery was not going to work. Everything we had done to try to support her in traditional ways and from a place of authority to try to get her back on track were harming, not helping, her. With all our best intentions, we were making things worse.

> This illness was changing Issy and we also had to change if we were going to help her. She couldn't be nudged back on the path she was on before mental illness. She wasn't going back anywhere – she had to go somewhere new and we had to join her.

How we would respond to Issy and how we could modify our behaviour were questions for her whole life, not just the next week or term. This was her illness and her future, not just a tick box or something we could overlook so everyone else (including us as parents) fell into line and had an easy life. Issy was seriously ill, yet it seemed that the most important thing for the professionals wasn't Issy's views or what was best for her recovery, but a focus on forcing her back into structures that had not supported her mental health in the first place. When we expected her to conform or adhere to rules from a life before mental illness, we disconnected and her mental health got worse. We set her back weeks or months. When we explored the options together, when we listened and stopped being the 'authority' on her, our bond grew and she felt safe enough to explore her illness. When we took the pressure off, recovery became an option.

We had to find a new way forward for us all. 'Partnering' – the approach we took that you can find out more about in Chapters 6 and 7 – became the way we connected with Issy and supported her through her illness.

It took a wholesale change in us as parents to help Issy get well again. It was hard and challenging to go against the behaviours and authority we had come to rely upon as parents, but, as we began to see Issy respond, we knew that it was the right thing for us all.

In the rest of the book I will share how we supported Issy to a resilient recovery and how important you are to your child getting well. I will show you there is hope and that you can find a way forward together; that you can come through this, with a stronger relationship with your child, your family, and yourself.

2

Is This All My Fault?

'Is this all my fault?' is a question that I spent far too much time trying to answer in the early stages of my daughter's illness. Maybe you're asking it too, as you try to understand and make sense of this unexpected and unwanted situation.

It's a natural response as a parent to take responsibility for everything to do with our child. We often enjoy the applause for their highs and then carry the blame for their lows. So when something as challenging as mental illness happens, blaming ourselves can be the quickest, safest and most 'logical' response. We can't imagine something as desperate as this happening without us being involved in some major way.

In a poll in the Parenting Mental Health Facebook group, 94.7 per cent of parents said they had blamed themselves for their child's mental health difficulties. So it's not just you, or me in 2015. It's a very natural feeling. But it's not necessarily a true one.

You might feel that a definitive and detailed answer to the question of responsibility can give you a sense of why and how you got here, and offer up a shortcut to the control you feel you need to grasp what's going on and to begin to fix things. So let's look at that now.

It's not that simple

Your child, and their mental health, is complex. And as parents, we are not in control of, or privy to, our child's thoughts. We can't know the reasons behind how or why they respond in the ways they do. We're not in their minds. We are not them. While there may be specific, traumatic circumstances to reflect upon, there will also be a patchwork of situations, experiences, reactions and responses that will have brought your child to this point. You are not responsible for, or in control of, all of them.

> Based on current population figures and World Health Organization (WHO) data, there are in the world between 326 million and 653 million young people under 25 suffering with a mental disorder. The WHO defines 'mental disorders' as emotional disorders, such as depression and anxiety, behavioural disorders, such as ADHD, eating disorders, psychosis, suicide and self-harm.

There are broader factors that will have influenced your child's mental health – people and situations and emotions that they didn't know how to deal with. It's important to consider this if we are going to release some of the responsibility and ownership of our child's mental illness and be in a position to really support them. In this chapter, we'll look at some of the events that may have shaped your child's mental health and its decline.

This is not meant to give you an answer to the question of whose fault this is or to fill your head with what you 'coulda, woulda, shoulda' done. It is to give you an awareness and understanding of what might have got you here and what might keep you here.

Before we do this, let's explore *that* question.

Is This All My Fault?

The question of my culpability consumed every waking moment, and many sleeping moments too, after Issy had disclosed her plan to end her life. It chattered constantly at me as we made our way through the daily agenda of psychiatric appointments, medication and care. It demanded attention when I was mindlessly washing up or stirring the dinner. It took advantage of the quiet of the night, when the house was at rest, or as I began to hear a kind whisper in my head, doing its best to soothe me. It was at its most potent and damaging when I was feeling tentatively hopeful or trying to take positive action. Was it something we as parents had done or not done? All thoughts led to it being my fault. If I could only understand what I'd done to make her ill, maybe I could do the opposite and speed her recovery.

I found myself turning over situations, reactions and memories in search of the clue that would give me the answers. Was it because I had worked when she was growing up? Or not listened enough? Or said no in 2007, or yes in 2009, or maybe in 2014? I was desperate to find the root cause and yet, I simply couldn't.

When we engaged with CAMHS, the Child Adolescent Mental Health Services, one of their early actions was to interview us as parents, together and then alone. Finding out whether we were part of the problem is a completely reasonable and understandable strategy to employ, but it added to the shady sense in my mind that this was all my fault.

Yet the more we engaged with CAMHS and delved into the why of the situation, I saw that I was stuck in a moment, trying to answer an unanswerable question. The reasons behind Issy's mental illness weren't simple and they weren't all mine to own. Not only was the notion that I was solely to blame not helpful for her, it wasn't true. This was her illness, and the range of reasons for it couldn't simply be packaged up and labelled 'Mr & Mrs Alderson's'.

And gradually, just as I had realised this was not my fault, and not my illness to fix or own, I realised that the question I had been wrestling with was not mine to answer either. It wasn't helpful, and it wasn't helping. I needed to stop asking that question for Issy's sake and, instead, focus on understanding what had impacted and what was still impacting on her, in order to be a better support.

It was only when I looked deeper that I began to see that I wasn't to blame, as you aren't either. The best way forward was to stop believing that taking responsibility would in some way help Issy. It was time to try to understand the world through her eyes and focus my attention on understanding the triggers, both external and in our home, that exacerbated her mental ill health.

'Mum, you were my rock, you were my best friend. I could always rely on you. I got angry and emotional because I was ill, but I never blamed you for what you had or hadn't done. I never saw you as someone who was trying to hurt me or undermine me. You were always totally there for me.'

Issy

Shifting the Blame

Like me, you might never know exactly why your child became ill in that moment. There are many external, biological and environmental factors impacting on them, many of which we have little to no control over, as well as this being a time of enormous emotional, physical and hormonal change, and we are going to look at some of those now.

I've learned from my experience, and from those of the parents in the Parenting Mental Health community, that a fixation on trying to make sense of why now and why us isn't always helpful when it comes to mental illness. It can lead us to an unhealthy focus on one thing, like gaming, social media or a poor diet, all in pursuit of blame. Making something else the root cause can feel definitive and definite, and give us that feeling of control that can be so elusive in this time of complete uncertainty. But that approach can isolate us further from our child, because, so often, those things are a coping mechanism or just something they get pleasure from at a time when feeling good is hard.

Challenging times

Situations that unsettle the status quo, remove the certainty that can come from close relationships and routine, or diminish the sense of control, certainty or safety a young person feels can all impact on mental well-being. The list of factors that can have an impact on mental health is long:

- sexual, emotional or physical abuse
- the death of a loved one
- divorce
- changing schools
- a friend moving away
- the loss of a job
- a break-up
- a new sibling

- your new partner
- crimes such as burglary or assault

Bullying was a trigger for Issy's mental state to decline rapidly and, sadly, she is not alone.

> According to the anti-bullying charity Ditch the Label, one-fifth of young people in the UK have been bullied in the last year, with 75 per cent saying it affected their mental health and 50 per cent saying they became depressed.

Physical health

Another potential challenge to a young person's mental health can come from neurological disorders and underlying health conditions. Autism – a lifelong developmental disorder – can be accompanied by mental health issues. According to ADAA, the Anxiety and Depression Association of America, '40 per cent of young people with ASD have clinically elevated levels of anxiety or at least one anxiety disorder, including obsessive compulsive disorder.'

Living with long-term conditions like postural orthostatic tachycardia syndrome (PoTS) or type 1 diabetes takes a psychological toll on young people that can lead to increased mental health issues. Research completed by Michele Yeo, an adolescent physician, and Professor Susan Sawyer found that: 'chronically ill young people are more likely . . . to have a lower level of emotional well-being than their healthy peers. Young people often report a sense of alienation from their peers and frustration with the requirements of managing their condition and negotiating the healthcare system.'

Childhood cancer can also have a similar impact on adolescent mental health. CLIC Sargent's report, 'Hidden Costs', found that 79 per cent of young people felt cancer had a serious impact on their emotional well-being, with 70 per cent of young people experiencing depression and 90 per cent of young people experiencing anxiety during their cancer treatment.

> The number of children and young people attending A&E in the UK with a psychiatric condition has more than doubled since 2009 and, in the past three years, hospital admissions for teenagers with eating disorders have also almost doubled.

All in the genes?

And we can't overlook genetic predisposition when it comes to answering the question of why we're here, but we also shouldn't use it as either a stick to beat ourselves with or a definitive reason for our child's mental health decline. Both my husband and I have suffered with mental health issues, but Issy's big brother hasn't. It isn't a given, and the research backs this up. The research paper, 'Genetics factors in major depression disease', by Maria Shadrina, Elena A. Bondarenko and Petr A. Slominsky, found that while 'family and twin studies have demonstrated that the contribution of genetic factors to the risk of the onset of DD [Depressive Disease] is quite large ... in most cases, these associations have not been confirmed in replication studies, and only a small number of genes have been proven to be associated with DD development risk.' Look at genetic predisposition as a potential warning, rather than a guarantee.

According to the WHO, rates of depression and anxiety among teenagers have increased by 70 per cent in the past 25 years. Worldwide, 10–20 per cent of children and adolescents experience mental disorders. Half of all mental illnesses begin by the age of 14 and three-quarters by mid-twenties.

A different world

There is no doubt that the world my children have grown up in is very different to the one that I did. Not in a rose-tinted, nostalgia-laden way, but in practical terms. The access they have to the world, to information and to others they've never met goes way beyond the *Encyclopaedia Britannica* and pen pal from exotic Torquay of my youth. The access the world has to *them* is beyond my wildest dreams. They're effectively living out *The Truman Show*, while we could close our front doors and hide under the duvet reading Judy Blume.

But, unlike the bubble of *The Truman Show*, they're being fed a diet of expectation and information beyond their young experience; expectations around body image, sexuality and sexual activity, what success looks like, what failure looks like, and what they *should* do and be. And it's difficult to ignore the potential impact this deluge of information may have on their mental well-being.

The WHO states that suicide is the single leading cause of death among adolescents in the low- and middle-income countries of the WHO European Region. Not car crashes or drugs, not accidents or cancer, but a deep, internal illness that is invisible to the eye. Suicide is the second leading cause of death among 15–29-year-olds globally.

In an always-on world, there's little escape, FOMO (fear of missing out) and insufficient space to process events, feelings and emotions. The influences on our children aren't just in their immediate environment; they're the teenager their age who is a YouTube millionaire, the influencers, the people they've never met who suddenly hold the key to their thoughts and choices. When people look like they live a perfect life, it's a hard standard to live up to, however much we explain or our children understand that it's not real. The picture-perfect, one-dimensional images that spill into our minds from our devices don't tend to show negative emotion or seek to embrace it. And the always-on access to all means of expression – from make-up tutorials to self-harm guides – can overload young people. It's worth noting, though, that it isn't all bad, and I will look at how social media and gaming can offer a sense of belonging to some in Chapter 12 (see page 237).

The teenage brain

The teenage years are hard work; deciding who we are, what we believe and what is important to us while our brains and bodies develop. The teenage brain is making intensive and crucial changes to itself in adolescence, leading to experimentation in decision-making, risk-taking and experience.

Chartered psychologist Zanneta Neale explains: 'Some of the most important changes to the brain that happen during adolescence include removal of excessive neural connections and increases in white matter. This is the portion of brain matter that allows different regions to communicate with one another. The teenage brain is unique and, therefore, due to this stage of development, the teenage years are a time when we are particularly sensitive and potentially vulnerable.'

The pruning of grey matter starts at the back of the brain, meaning the prefrontal cortex, where decision-making, consideration of consequences, problem-solving and impulse control happen, changes last. This leads to teenagers relying more on the amygdala, a part of the brain associated with emotions and instinctive reactions.

According to Tony Jurich, who was professor of family studies and human services at Kansas State University, 'teens think they are invincible. So when they feel psychological pain, they are more apt to feel overwhelmed by hopelessness and the belief that they have no control over their lives.'

The teenage brain, by its changing nature, can reinforce extremes of good and bad, making it vulnerable to stressors and leading to higher rates of poor mental health.

A Better Question

There are lots of factors that can lead to poor mental health, many of which are out of the control and remit of a parent. Taking responsibility for the reasons why 'because that's what parents do' isn't helpful to your mental health or to your child's. It can leave you in a state of blame and shame that limits your ability to support your child effectively and to see what might help or hinder their progress.

Your child's experience of life is different to yours, and not recognising events or factors that have caused them mental distress can invalidate their experience and keep them isolated and in pain. To begin to understand that pain, we must look beyond the stories we tell ourselves about our role and what has happened. Instead of asking, 'Is this my fault?' why not ask, 'What can the reasons behind my child's mental health issues teach me?' and 'How can they show me how best to support my child?'

Keep in mind . . .

1. It's not your fault! There are lots of reasons why your child may become mentally ill.
2. You're not alone. Sadly, this is happening to millions of families around the world.
3. Lose the guilt! It can be counterproductive in helping your child to recover. Your understanding of the potential factors is more helpful to your child than you taking on the blame unnecessarily.

3

Everything Changes

As Issy's reactions and behaviours changed, and as what was possible for her began to reduce radically, I had no answers. Looking back, my strategies before she became suicidal weren't working and neither was pretending it wasn't happening. I felt complete despair, total desperation and a sense that we were completely, utterly alone. I struggled to accept the 'new normal' we faced, and I was fighting with strategies that had worked on a life before mental illness.

Though it may have been alarming at an already challenging time, and I might not have been in a position to hear it in all its brutal glory, I wish someone had held my hand and shared what was to be expected and what was to come. For all the probable pain, it would have given me a small sense of comfort – that I could brace myself for whatever came next, however unbelievable, inconceivable or savage it may have seemed then. And then I could have begun to trust myself a little more. I could have put away the 'quilt of guilt' that I'd wrapped myself in, as a way to find solution, comfort and certainty. It would have given me permission to see the situations I faced as usual for that unusual time and not a pure judgement on my parenting.

In this chapter, I hope to share some of the impacts of mental illness, what your 'new normal' might feel like and what power you have in this extraordinary time. While we may not be able to pre-empt all the impacts, and you probably won't be able to change them on your own, I hope that, at the very least, you won't be quite as surprised or filled with shame as I was when they happen.

The Impact on Your Child

Your child may have been wrestling with their mental health in the confines of their own mind for a long time before the impact was felt by you and the family. Every day your child has woken up and wondered what is and isn't possible. It's frightening to see your potential decreasing in front of your eyes. So, the sooner we can acknowledge their mental health issues, the faster we can begin to build a safe space for our child to explore and deal with their illness.

It's hard at times to distinguish between mental health issues and what some might call teenage behavioural issues. For me, all behaviour is communication. Our children are fighting to find a way to share their fears and emotions when they are angry or sensitive. When they withdraw or become frustrated, there can be a number of reasons that don't add up to naughtiness, defiance or belligerence. They may be trying to process what they're facing and might not have the words to explain it. They might not have the capacity to deal with *our* emotions as well as theirs, however loving we are, or they may not want to burden us. What we may see as unwanted behaviour may be our child's only way of responding to what they feel. They are ultimately seeking connection, not correction or attention, when their mental health is challenging them.

I asked Issy to tell me how she remembers the slide into mental illness and what it felt like for her:

'I started having more and more bad days, but I thought that eventually as I got older things might get better. It seemed like a war of attrition, and I struggled to just keep pushing through. As time went on, bad days became bad weeks and I didn't think it was going to ever get any better. When the causes of depression are around you the whole time – people or things bigger than you that are completely out of your control – it's very overwhelming and I felt it was my fault. Being bullied made me feel helpless and eventually I fell off the edge.'

The early signs of mental ill health

As the bad days blend into a bad month and onwards, there are many ways that young people try to change the cycle or slow it down; new behaviours are an attempt to take control of the elements of their lives that they can. Changing hairstyles, getting tattoos, drinking alcohol, smoking and taking drugs are all ways of trying to change the state they are in. Increased anger, crying or unreasonable reactions can all be ways of trying to exert some power, to prove to themselves that they still have agency over themselves and their life.

Repetitive behaviours are another form of control. Maybe your child has started a new routine? Whether it's having to do certain things before they leave the house, like making their bed or wearing a certain top, or seemingly positive behaviours, such as extra studying or a strict fitness regimen, this could be an example of trying to take control and gain some certainty.

Irritability is a common output of changing mental health states. Yes, as parents we are intrinsically annoying to teenagers – it's part of our job description. But when the irritability between parents and children becomes new and intense, it's not just 'usual teen behaviour'.

Issy taught me early on that constant questioning of her state would lead to extreme irritability, and that it was not helpful because it exacerbated her feelings of 'not being OK'. Asking someone what is wrong when they can't answer the question may appear as an act of love to us, but it is undermining and can sabotage trust.

Irritability can lead to withdrawal, both physically and emotionally. It may be used by a teen to shield themselves from the overwhelming fear of a situation, or it may be to protect you from the pain of their thoughts. They may not want to converse with you in case they inadvertently leave you with the darkness that they're carrying around. They may not be able to cope as you try to make them see that 'it's not that bad after all', when it really, really is. Or they may change their mind seemingly without notice, when actually they've been debating the situation for days or weeks.

Conversely, your child may turn towards you more. They may see you as their safe space, and not want to leave your side. The everyday privacy and autonomy we have come to expect with our children growing up – like heading to the toilet alone or waking up on our terms – can diminish, or even disappear, when our child is in crisis.

Seeking validation is common in teenagers (and, let's be honest, humans) and, when everything you know has changed, it becomes even more important. Issy says she felt more vulnerable when she was mentally ill and needed more reassurance that she was OK, because she didn't know if she was. Issy would look to me for validation and this gave us an opportunity to connect. Your child may instead lean on friends or people you don't know to get this sense of comfort.

As a parent juggling so many things, it can be easy to see our child in simplistic terms, and forget that this human being is a complex mix of changing hormones, beliefs, opinions and ideals, unique in their make-up and more special than they will ever appreciate. They have the same fears, hopes and dreams as we did at their age, and are battling to make sense of a rush of change and challenge. When we try to neaten up their experiences, or judge them for the behaviours they are using to gain a sense of control, or diminish their experience because it isn't easy or nice, we compact the issues and send them further underground.

> The way your child is acting may seem different or unacceptable to you, but please try to look beyond it. Initially, they are trying to make sense of what is going on and gain some control. Whatever that looks like, we may not understand it. We may try to manage it, but that won't help them or the relationship.

Challenging behaviour is your child's way of trying to cope and make sense of what is going on. It's not an attack on you, an affront to all you've done for them or a choice. Please don't treat them differently for it. See it as an opportunity to understand. They didn't learn how to feel this bad on social media, they didn't catch it from their friends and this isn't just 'being a teenager'; it's being a human.

The Impact on You

Supporting a child with a mental illness challenges all we know and believe about ourselves as a parent. It also changes our priorities and perceptions of what is important. It calls us to examine what and who we need in our lives and how we view situations. It questions our beliefs, our resolve and our resilience. It is a brutal awakening, if we choose to be woken by it. But it is a powerful and brave choice to experience the rainbow of emotions that come from this extraordinary time.

It can be the beginning of a deeply personal transformation, and one that not many of us are blessed to experience. It might not feel like it, but you're a member of a very special club now!

I'm not sure if I can describe the sense of dread and fear and deep sadness I felt when Issy became suicidal. It felt as if nothing mattered anymore, except keeping her alive at any cost. In one solitary moment, when the doctor called me to say my daughter was going to end her life imminently, everything I thought I knew and had control over disappeared.

Mental illness keeps you stuck in a moment. It brings a sense that life is on pause and, while the rest of the world continues in technicolour, you fade into a monochrome existence that doesn't change and that no one sees. And this is a very real feeling and one you have every right to resent.

You may feel anger at what is going on or maybe at the reason why you believe your child has been affected. You might feel frustrated that you can't change things. You might feel sad and disconnected and that you no longer recognise your child and haven't the faintest idea how to reach them and help them through this dark time. These are all normal and natural feelings.

Many of us parents caring for a child with a mental illness become depressed, because the overwhelming burden and caring 24/7 takes an emotional toll we aren't ready to cope with. We can feel isolated from the world and, with that, detached from a sense of perspective that might help us see that we need to take care of ourselves too.

I wasn't expecting to have to give up the life I knew, who I thought I was, what I could do, my job, my freedom, for this newer, harder, more demanding, more difficult time, but as I did I found a new type of resolve and strength. I found my voice and advocated hard to ensure that the care Issy got was right for her. I wouldn't back down when I was challenged on something I was passionate about. I wouldn't entertain things that before I'd have agreed with through gritted teeth.

It took me about 12 months to come to terms with Issy's illness and reconcile my part in it, good and bad. I found it highly emotional going back to familiar places she could no longer access, such as driving past her old school for the first time and howling like a baby for everything she'd had to go through. Letting go can be hard, and it takes time and kindness to work its way out of our hearts.

Your child's mental illness will undoubtedly impact on you, and it's so important to be kind to yourself as you navigate and hopefully embrace these changes. Look at the chapter on self-care (Chapter 9, page 147) for more reasons about why you matter and how to support yourself in this time.

This experience has the power to take away everything you know about yourself and your life, but it also offers you a chance for something completely new to fill its place.

Believe it or not, it is offering you an opportunity – to know yourself better and to know your child better. It is a chance to challenge unhelpful or damaging assumptions and expectations, and to build a different kind of strength and resilience that only comes when the most precious thing to you has been threatened.

The Impact on Family Life

Your child's mental illness has an impact beyond them. It influences the kinds of conversations you have as a family, it challenges the things you can do – like holidays and family get-togethers, school and work – and it will change the shape of your life. It sounds dramatic and, I'm sad to say, it is.

The continuous uncertainty begins to invade your own sense of peace and makes you fearful and pre-emptive, and unable to make plans. Appointments are broken, invitations turned down and connections lessened. Before you know it, life doesn't look or feel like it used to at all, and you're not quite sure how that happened and have no idea whether or when circumstances will ever change. You approach people and plans with trepidation. Your family may try to keep some sense of normality, but you're overwhelmed by how this life happened to you.

And if dealing with our own emotions wasn't enough, we have to deal with the adjustments and uncertainty that mental illness brings to siblings, grandparents and friends, and manage those too. It's exhausting. Siblings don't understand that behaviour you wouldn't normally tolerate is suddenly 'OK'. You become a master mediator, trying to manage each child's needs while keeping them connected. It can feel as if your family will never be the same again.

When your child is first ill, you might think it's just *their* relationships with friends, teachers or other family members that are challenged. Sadly, this isn't the case, and you'll see the impact of coping with an open-ended illness, without rules or prognosis, clouding your relationships with friends, family, work and, perhaps most importantly, yourself.

The Impact on Your Relationship

If you have a partner, they may be on side during this experience, or not. They may get what's going on, or feel aggrieved that you're focusing all your energy on your child. They may feel that it's a behavioural issue that can be disciplined away. They may be struck by the same feelings you may hold – fear, guilt, failure. My husband, Ross, and I fought Issy's illness together, shoulder to shoulder, but in very different ways. While we remained resolute in our focus, many of the grumbles and gripes we had were nothing to do with what we thought they were. They were expressions of our fear that spilled over and came out as everyday frustrations about who didn't wash up or put the bins out. (It was him, of course!) We didn't have the emotional reserves to offer each other as much of the space and understanding that we normally do. We didn't have the language to express how we felt. We were together, but alone, trying to make sense of what was going on, both looking at it from different perspectives.

There is more on working with your partner in Chapter 10 (page 182).

The Impact Beyond Your Home

If we're struggling to make sense of some of the new behaviours while we live with our children, it can be equally hard, in a different way, for extended family and friends who are getting a mere snapshot of events without any context.

Relationships that have always followed a certain rhythm can be thrown into chaos: Granny doesn't understand why little Jimmy doesn't want to come round on Sunday and won't let it go – maybe you've not wanted to worry her with the facts of his anxiety and that he now can't leave the house. Your friends stop asking you to join them, knowing you can't leave your child, and then stop calling because they don't know what to say, and neither do you.

There is a tendency to gloss over mental illness, in part because of prevailing stigmas surrounding it, but also because we're not generally used to having the kinds of deep, emotionally vulnerable conversations that tend to be needed when we discuss our child's mental health challenges. I felt that no one really understood what we were going through when Issy became ill. It was uncharted territory and our usual support network of family and friends simply didn't have the tools to help us. It felt as if love and compassion wasn't enough, because without an understanding of the constant fear of finding Issy dead, of the dread that permeated every day and stole away our hope for the future, how could they really understand? In some cases, they couldn't see the severity of the situation or the relevance of certain actions. One friend laughed at a situation at school that had kept Issy awake and anxious for three nights. It wasn't meant to be mean, it was simply that they didn't understand the power of small actions to challenge any sense of stability.

'My friends and family were alarmed when I told them about J's illness. They were obviously thinking that it must be terrible and probably glad it wasn't them. The problem I found is that it becomes a one-way street. You tell them horrible things and all they can do is provide platitudes because they don't have the experience or context to help, so you begin to feel awkward. You come away with nothing other than the feeling that you might have burdened them with something they can't do anything about, rather than feeling you've shared a problem, and halved it. So I stopped talking to them about it. It was too painful.'

R, parent of 14-year-old

Mental illness can take the strongest of bonds and force you to see things in another person that you haven't ever been in a situation to see before. You may find your partner, ex-partner, grandparent, boss or friend hasn't got the same views as you about what is going on. You may see their appraisal of the situation as heartless and hurtful and be unable to look beyond it. You may simply not be able to find it in yourself to see their point of view. Or you may find new and special connections with people you have previously been distanced from. Mental illness brings out extraordinary things in us, both good and bad. See Chapter 11 (page 194) for more ways to handle friends and family.

Recognising the 'New Normal'

Before I could begin to properly support my daughter and appreciate the changes that mental illness brought to our relationships, practicalities and plans, I had to come to terms with this 'new normal' we faced. And I can't lie, it was really, really challenging.

Giving up the routines, responsibilities and freedoms of my life so that they could be replaced with life-threatening challenge, uncertainty, fear, grief, guilt ... who wants that? Certainly not me c. 2015 and I denied it for as long as I could before Issy became suicidal, and struggled with it once she was in crisis. But crisis changed my perception of what we faced. Instead of fighting to force life back into the shape it had been before, I realised that this couldn't be cajoled back. It wasn't a shape I knew and I didn't have the authority to force it.

The 'new normal' is the brutal and much-changed reality we face when mental illness comes into our family. It's the harsh reality we probably don't want, because it challenges us, our relationships, our hopes, our expectations and our strength. And it's a very human and natural response to ignore it or overlook it for as long as possible. But, we need to embrace the new normal if we are going to help our child through, help build self-belief and agency in them, and forge a bond that goes beyond mental illness.

I'm afraid that the new normal is here to stay whether you like it or not, and it needs you to understand that the rules have changed. It needs you to step up and into this new place for your family, however much you don't want to. It needs you to see what is going on and embrace its uncertainty and darkness. It needs you to acknowledge the current challenges and understand it so you can make it easier for your child, and your family.

Recognising grief

According to the Grief Recovery Method, grief is defined as 'the conflicting feelings caused by the end of or change in a familiar pattern of behaviour'. We often associate grief only with death, divorce or other life-changing experiences. But we can feel the same intense and overwhelming sense of loss when our child becomes mentally ill. The emotional and often physical pain is as real as if we'd lost a loved one.

When we are living with the physical person, but not with the psychological make-up we're used to, we can be suffering from 'ambiguous loss', a form of grief defined by Pauline Boss in the seventies, where there is no clear ending or closure.

We are grieving for a life we had expected to live, for the hopes and aspirations that we held for our child, and by default for ourselves; we are mourning the freedoms and potential of a future we had planned and anticipated, but hadn't yet lived. We are grieving the loss of control, of the feeling that we are in charge, that we have power and agency to make change happen.

We may find ourselves denying the emotions we feel around the loss of the person we knew or find ourselves with conflicting feelings. When we reflect on the jarring nature of discovering our perfect child is self-harming or so anxiety-ridden that they become almost a stranger, we can often overlook the loss, in favour of trying to change the present. If we can just stop them hurting themselves or encourage them to try to engage, we won't have to fully embrace the pain of change.

And it's not just around changes to your child. We can grieve the loss of our life as we knew it. It's easy to look back at life before mental illness and wonder where you went and why you can't get back to the 'you' you knew.

While it's not as visible as a death or major life change, we should treat ourselves as gently as if we had lost a loved one. Lower your expectations, allow yourself to feel and explore the injustice, anger, frustration, or whatever comes up for you. Talk about why you feel as you do.

Things won't be the same again, and that is OK. Kindly allowing yourself to reflect on the things that have changed and won't happen again can create space for different experiences to develop. What can you learn from your grief? What are your most important values? What are your non-negotiables?

Letting go of the life we had and expected is hard, but it's important to let go of the past, even if we can't yet embrace the new. What can you let go of? It might be people, places, expectations or ideals. How can you appreciate what you have now?

And we should expect that others around us are grieving too; maybe not in the same way or on the same timescale, but they will be feeling their own sense of loss. Being compassionate and gentle, even when we don't see their point of view, can lead to a kinship that transcends perspective but is grounded in understanding.

Are you prepared to adapt?

The new normal is like a reset button. No, you didn't ask for it, but someone or something pressed it. It resets all your previous preferences – everything from where you go on holiday to whether you can concentrate to whether you will all be able to go to your friend's at the weekend.

But it's not easy letting go of things you love, things that define you, hopes, dreams, plans and routines. It takes patience, time and love to counter the resistance, frustration and anger you may feel. It's not something we can simply switch on or off; it's a process and needs compassion. Letting go of anything we love is a process that we have to revisit if we're going to make peace with it, and embracing the new normal is no different. That's why it's so important we take care of ourselves and our own mental health.

It's only from the passage of time that I realised that I had to grieve so much, to enable me to make sense of what we were facing and to begin to look with a hint of optimism to the new future. I held expectations of Issy's life and I had to let them go. While none of us can guarantee the future, before mental illness, I had a slight arrogance that, as a parent, I was in some kind of control of its direction. I'm not sure I was in any kind of control really, but it was a belief I held and had to let go of.

I held expectations about myself, and I had to reflect on them and challenge their truth; my ability to control things, my value as a parent, my own emotional strength and resilience.

I held expectations about the future, for us as a family. What did this mean for our future? What would it look like? Did we have one?

On a more practical level, I didn't expect to have to deal with my own sense of failure when I couldn't cope with everything I normally juggled, or when my brain wouldn't engage or find the right words and all I could do was think of Issy wanting to end her life. I had to work through the associated guilt of letting people down, while dealing with the emotional fallout of my daughter being on suicide watch. It doesn't make sense as I write it now, but, at the time, these kinds of expectations weighed heavily on me. It is as if the reality of our child's mental health decline sneaks up on us and our emotional response to it takes time to catch up and process it.

Learning the 'new rules'

When we entered the crisis stage of Issy's illness, it almost felt as if there was a set of new, unspoken rules. It took me a lot of time and a whole heap of heartache to learn these. If someone could have written them down for me, it would have really helped. And so, here they are:

1. You can't fix this. That's not your job.
2. Forget what you think you know. This needs a new approach.
3. You're not to blame, but you can have an impact and influence – good and bad. Feeling guilty will harm your mental health and your child's, so let that go.
4. Take one day at a time. If that's too much, take one hour, one minute or one second.
5. You and your behaviours are the blueprint for your child. Assume positive intent – it makes every interaction easier for everyone.
6. Self-care is fuel, not indulgence (see Chapter 9). Being kind to yourself is as important as breathing.
7. Not everyone will understand and that's OK. Find those who do.
8. Patience is a superpower.
9. It's OK to not be OK. You matter too.
10. The only certainty is your ability to cope.
11. Believe – in your child and their bright, brilliant future; in yourself; in the possibility of change. And if you can't – pretend! Your mind will catch up.
12. If at any time you feel that you cannot keep your child safe, take them to A&E. It's not a waste of time. It's their life.

There Is Always Hope

When you first face the shocking truth of your child's mental illness, the scale of the challenge ahead is inconceivable and it can feel that it's above your pay grade as a parent to deal with it. We're so used to having to have all the answers and, when we're faced with such a challenge, it can be a shock that we don't know what to do for the best.

Ross and I saw early on that we had an essential part to play in helping Issy through; not only in being supportive and understanding, but by using the pause that mental illness placed on our life to reflect on what we could change and do better to help her. One of the benefits of this change in approach was a connection with Issy that I could have only dreamed of and an understanding of myself and my family that has been transformational. It took time, it wasn't pretty or easy, but I'm not sure anything worthwhile is.

Issy's mental illness, despite the pain of it, was a true gift of adversity. It gave me the opportunity to change my mindset and see that, despite all I couldn't control, I had enormous power as a parent to influence the duration and severity of her illness and build the strongest, sweetest bond with her.

You have some power here

You have control over your mindset, the words you use, the expectations you hold and the way you show love and direction. And, in turn, these will impact on your child and how they make their way through. You have an opportunity to create a bond with your child, and yourself, that you couldn't possibly have done outside of this experience. You have a chance to help your child build a level of resilience at a young age that many people don't get in their lifetime. You have a chance to share with them the tools for being a good human – how to love themselves, how to respect themselves, and how to love and respect others. You get a chance to help them build a strength, knowledge and understanding of themselves, and to show them how to be self-compassionate, in the face of extreme challenge. The skills you share with your child in this time will influence their self-esteem, their self-worth and future relationships (including those with any potential future grandchildren).

This life-challenging and life-changing event comes with two options: stay as you are, or evolve. While evolution can feel painful, staying where you are will hurt more in the longer term.

I can't say it won't be hard – the experience of the past five years still has the power to bring me to tears. But we are stronger than we thought possible and we are changed people for it. Whether your child makes you feel that you are important in their life or not, let me tell you that you are. You have a vital role to play in their illness and in their recovery.

You may feel grief at what you have lost and despair at what might come, but there is such a lot for you to gain. And even though everything feels uncertain and you might not know quite where you are going, when you get there, you'll meet a strong, resilient and robust version of yourself, if you can let it happen.

Keep in mind . . .

1. The impacts of mental illness are far-reaching and challenging.
2. Embracing the 'new normal' can ease the pain of this time.
3. This adversity is an opportunity for you and your family to evolve.

4

Your Emotional Response

In this chapter we are going to look at how you (and your partner) are handling this in more detail. It is OK to be scared, and it is completely normal and human to be frightened now. I hope that by sharing some of what I felt and by identifying some of what you might be experiencing, it may help you feel that it's OK to feel what you do. You're not alone.

Facing the Big Emotions

The mental and emotional clarity I was so in need of to help me determine my next move and come to terms with the 'new normal' was often challenged by a surfeit of overwhelm. Big emotions, like guilt or shame, along with a deep sadness that I couldn't shrug off, took over my attention, when I really wanted to focus on my daughter. Making sense of why I felt so isolated and disconnected wasn't a high priority at the time, but reflecting on some of the emotions I was feeling would have helped me process them sooner. Hopefully this will help you now, whatever stage you are at.

So much of parenting is about balancing optimism, blind faith and bravado to muddle through. Whatever issue or problem we face, we can tell ourselves we have it covered, because we're parents. This gives us a feeling of courage we're not sure we really own, but we muster to stand by our decisions and be consistent. So, it's a really brave act to face your fears as a parent of a young person with a mental health issue. There are two main thoughts here: facing your fears about what might happen for your child, and also facing your fears around what you might have contributed through your behaviour or response. It's never nice to recognise where we've made mistakes, but, if you can, it will put you in a stronger position to help your child through whatever may come, and it will help you to support them, and yourself, better.

Feelings of shock and fear

That moment when you are told that your child's unusual or disturbing behaviour is because of a mental illness and you realise you can't love mental illness away, your brain is flooded with unanswerable questions and unhelpful judgements. That initial jolt of shock and emotion may be something that you and those around you process differently. My husband wanted to fix it. 'What can we do?' he asked, when I told him our daughter had a plan to end her life. I, instead, walked around like a zombie, emotionally empty from the shock of what I had been told.

The greatest fear of a parent is to lose a child, through death. I can't shy away from the subject of suicide here. We have to speak its name so that we can unpick and uncover the reasons behind its growth. I don't have the words to describe what it is like to face the prospect of losing a child to suicide. I am taken back to some of the most difficult and challenging days and some of the darkest and longest nights of my life. I've seen some tough times in my life but nothing compares to the feeling of despair and fear that the mention of suicide invokes.

When our children become suicidal, we find ourselves faced with a number of questions that are natural, but don't really help the urgency of the situation we face:

- What didn't we do?
- How could we have helped more?
- How did we miss it?
- How on earth did we get here?

As someone who sits five years away from that first diagnosis and first suicide attempt, I have to tell you that these questions are not helpful. Please write them down once, and then let them go with love and peace: burn them, tear them up, chuck them away. They don't help anyone, least of all you and your child. They are sent to steal away your energy, your hope and your presence. Fight them at all costs. You need to be strong, you need to be present and you need to believe that you can get through this.

> Forgiving yourself for being the beautiful and flawed human being that you are, who has done the best they could with what they knew at the time, will help you get through this extraordinary time in one piece.

Fear for the future

There were many days where I wondered if my daughter would ever be able to live independently; I wondered if she would ever be able to leave the house. I even considered how to remodel the house so her 30-something self would have a bit more space and privacy. Would she live in a world inhabited by only us, her parents, and whoever she met online?

All of the assumptions that our children will grow up, leave home and live independent, purposeful lives of their own are challenged during this time. These fears are very natural and are absolutely valid to have, but they will drain your energy if you try to live too far in the future.

Facing your fears is hard to do, because who wants to admit to their child being mentally ill or suicidal? But your fear can stop you from making good decisions around taking the next steps and finding support.

Talking about what you are afraid of might feel painful to you today, but it won't hurt you forever. The denial that Ross and I felt as parents, for much longer than I am happy to admit, held us back from understanding the extent of the challenges and the actions we needed to make to help our daughter.

Losing control

There were times when I felt completely incapable of effecting change at a time when I felt I absolutely needed to have some form of control. I needed that control because I was scared. I was scared about the future for my daughter. I was scared about the impact of her illness on our family. And I was scared that I wouldn't have the capability, skills or gumption to get us all through.

Our fears kept us tied to the expectations society has placed on us to conform. If you care about living the life you are expected to, then you'll keep doing what you believe is necessary to maintain that route. By facing our fears, we learned quickly that the rules we'd adhered to no longer applied to us. This extraordinary time gave us an opportunity to stand apart from some of the societal norms about education, how to live a purposeful life and even the hierarchical dynamic of our parent/daughter relationship. It freed us to reflect on what was needed in order to help our daughter deal with her illness and recover. We took her out of school for two years; we fought to get her the care she needed on her terms; and we decided we weren't going to place her back in the same environment and that things would change. We were able to begin to amend our behaviour and push back on some of the expectations and assumptions that the people around us were making of how to help her back to wellness and our choices around that.

Write down your fears

Pick up a notebook and write down all your fears. Be honest. If you are fearful that your child may never leave home, name that fear. If you are scared that you can't cope anymore, acknowledge that fear. If you are frightened that friends and family will shun you, own that fear. The sooner you do, the sooner you can start to make changes so that your fears don't become your reality or lead your behaviour. This process of 'journaling' can help your brain to process what you are going through at this time. You can keep the pages or tear them up – whatever you choose.

Feelings of guilt

As a parent, guilt – the sense of regret or responsibility for what we feel we didn't do correctly, did do wrongly or should have done sooner or better – can become a measurement of how good a parent we believe we are. We all wear the 'quilt of guilt' at some point and we need to learn how to deal with it in some way.

Some parents say that they feel guilty for 'failing' their child. I use quotation marks here because these are not my words or my judgement, and neither are they accurate. You haven't failed your child. But I know that sometimes it feels like that. We all did what we could at the time, with the facts, energy and tools we had to hand. As Maya Angelou says, 'When we know better, we do better.'

While guilt can help us to determine what is right and wrong, it can quickly become an energy and optimism drain that makes us feel worse than we already do when our child is mentally ill. We often associate guilt with not living up to certain standards, and putting our parenting up for inspection without changing our expectations leads to less energy, drive and belief in our power to support our child.

You might be feeling guilty for a number of reasons:

- Believing your actions are to blame and that you somehow gave permission for your child's mental health to decline.
- For not being able to change things because 'that's what parents should be able to do'.
- For being powerless to 'fix' this.
- For being too busy to see the signs.

The everyday can reinforce the sense of guilt we carry as we see our child struggling with the most usual of activities – having a shower, brushing their hair, sleeping on a typical schedule, going to school, going out with their friends, believing they have a future.

You may feel guilty for having to make medical or life decisions that are difficult and appear uncompassionate but are in your child's best interests; for not spending time with your other children or your family; for letting the side down at work; for spending time on yourself, for not listening, for assuming, for trying and not making the progress you'd hoped to, for losing the connection with the people you love the most. The list is endless.

Over time, if we don't recognise that we did the best we could, guilt can shift towards shame, where we can find ourselves believing we have created and enabled our child's illness and we are responsible for it all. We see our actions or inactions as being a sign of our innate weakness or that we're not the caring parent we thought we were. When this happens, it's often reassuring to wrap ourselves in the 'quilt of guilt', as a defence against a perceived lack of understanding and a surfeit of judgement. When we take responsibility for everything that is wrong, we can't be castigated or scrutinised, can we?

The problem with the 'quilt of guilt' is that it covers up all of the brilliant things you have done and all the compassionate actions and words that you have shared. It overlooks your best bits in favour of an overly harsh appraisal of yourself and locks out any opportunity for empathy, connection and love from others. And while that isn't helpful for your own mental health, it sure as mustard doesn't help your child or your family either.

Subsuming guilt into yourself alters the way you see the world and your capabilities for change begin to diminish. It's not helpful for your child to see you feeling bad for things that neither of you could control, and the expectation of taking guilt on can spread to them.

How to deal with guilt

- Lower your expectations of yourself.
- Realign what is 'normal' and see the good in your 'new normal'.
- Forgive yourself – you did the best you could for the right reasons.
- Anchor yourself in the present – the only thing you can change is your next action.

Feelings of isolation

The fear that surrounds mental health can take us away to a barren landscape, where no one gets it, where no one sees us or the pain our family is enduring. The injustice of our circumstances and the misunderstandings of those around us can leave us feeling deeply, desperately alone.

Taking care of your child, worrying about them and their future, and dealing with psychiatrists, therapists, school, work, family, friends, life . . . it all takes a huge amount of head space. It can become all-consuming and, when you see friends, you may want to talk about it and get their perspective on something your child, school or a medical professional has said or done. Many parents find that not everyone wants to hear about mental illness. In my opinion there is still a societal belief that 'poor parenting' creates the mental health issues we are seeing in young people. They may just not know what to say.

The feelings of isolation are completely normal. By sharing these feelings, we can begin to process the impact of caring on a daily and open-ended basis, and we can be validated that our responses are OK and wholly human. Community – both online and offline – is a great way to connect with individuals with shared experience. As C. S. Lewis wrote, 'Friendship is born at that moment when one person says to another: "What! You too? I thought I was the only one." ' I hear from many parents how powerful it is to find kinship, when someone sees your story and identifies with your struggle.

Nothing beats finding someone who has experienced or sensed the fear and worry you have. You don't have to know them well for this to be a powerful partnership. Some of the best interactions come where you don't really know the people you exchange your thoughts and feelings with. The very fact they understand because they are going through similar challenges, or have been through them, connects you in a unique way. And knowing you can vent, shout, rant and relieve yourself of the frustrations of your circumstances without reprisals, fear of judgement or reminders of words said in the heat of emotion, can bring a huge sense of calm to you.

Find your support network

Sharing your fears with people who have been there, who understand the gravity of the situation you face and who are prepared to hear them and say, 'Yes I felt/ thought/hated that too', is incredibly liberating. I would urge you to find support – whether that's a really sympathetic friend, a support group through your child's medical team or the Parenting Mental Health group (see page 295). I know that connecting with the amazingly supportive members there will help you see that your life isn't one big lump of despair. When you share your fears and emotions with others who get it, they lose a little of their power. They no longer hurt you as much, or dictate your response.

Say your fears out loud and you'll change the way you see them and they'll shrink to a manageable size. You've got other battles to fight.

You may feel isolated because your everyday life has changed. You may have had to give up things you enjoy, such as your job, hobbies or exercise sessions, or things like meeting a friend for coffee, because your life is chaotic and you don't know what's happening from one minute to the next, let alone days or even weeks in advance. Giving up the things that gift us space and peace isolates us by stealth – this week it might be that you can't go for coffee, and then you wake up and realise that you've cancelled the past three dates and your friend's calls are less frequent. It can be disconcerting and massively frustrating to see your support system falling away before your eyes, as other people, who don't have the skills or experience to connect with what you're going through, carry on living their lives. And it can lead you to feel rather bitter about the whole thing.

Again, this is so normal and you have every right to feel this way. But, stewing in isolation isn't good for any of us, so recognising this is happening and being patient with the illness and its impacts, as well as yourself, really helps.

Your emotions around what you're facing are really normal, and it's not only OK to explore them, it will help you become stronger and more able to cope with what is to come. It will give you a foundation so that you're able to approach your child's mental health challenges with the compassion and patience needed. We will cover this in more detail throughout the book.

Understanding Your Child's Behaviour

Partnering and parenting are long games, and remembering this helps when we are faced with less than acceptable behaviour. It's easy to see bad behaviour or verbal abuse as a personal attack – that your child disrespects you. When we see disrespect, it isn't easy to take your child's emotions and feelings into account. When you're in an emotionally charged situation, emotions and feelings override any logical or programmed responses, even in adulthood. And while it is hurtful and distressing, understand that your child is trying to take control of the forces that are acting upon them and wrangle some control into their world; you often are the target of their outbursts.

Your job is to be calm, to ensure they and you are safe, and to have perspective. It's easy to write that here, but not so easy to maintain when you're being bawled at day in and day out. But the simple act of understanding and not responding to it with the same behaviours that you're finding unacceptable may help you to diffuse the situation over time.

Another challenging situation is where children may try to escape that sense of powerlessness with drugs, alcohol, eating issues, self-harm, addiction to phones, physically running away or other behaviours. Complex as every person, relationship and family is, there is a reason behind every action. If you can have open, judgement-free conversations with your child and begin to discuss how and why they do a behaviour, while holding back your anger and frustration, you can start to excavate the reasons behind it.

You may not be able to have these conversations alone and may need the support of a professional, but acknowledging they are necessary, without judgement, is a gift to your child. From there, you can help the child to recognise the trigger and the need and they can begin to feel empowered and safe enough to make small shifts in how they respond. This is a long-term strategy, but you're not just trying to get them to stop harmful behaviours; you're trying to help them see they are powerful, they have choices in how they respond, how they spend their time and how they see themselves.

Judgement of our child

Judgement so easily slips out, unexpected and with no malice intended. Born from habit, it can be wrapped up in us wanting or expecting 'the best thing'. Generally, our judgement of our child comes from a place of judgement of ourselves. We can say it's for their benefit, but, underneath, the challenges may be:

- Why am I not in control?
- What is their behaviour doing to me?
- How is it impacting on my sense of order? On my life?
- What will it make people think of me?

Living by the unwritten tenets learned from our own experiences can certainly lead us to judgement. It is an immediate, reactive response and it exists because we believe that, as parents, we have authority and a right to exercise it, and that our way is the way. We may be literally or metaphorically yelling, 'Do as I say' to our child, when they simply can't. While it's so natural for our frustrations and fears to overflow, what our child really needs is for us to listen to what they need, rather than expect them to be in a place where they can do what we tell them.

> 'I just wanted him to do what I said, because I didn't know if I was strong enough to cope with his OCD and depression and I didn't want people to judge my parenting. As I stopped demanding things he couldn't do, I gradually felt less stressed about it all. I stopped thinking this was something he could control and it made it easier for us both.'
>
> J, parent of 17-year-old

Depression, along with many other mental disorders, is often based in powerlessness. When we, our family or our society, shuts down a child's right to process by ignoring or marginalising their right to feel, a feeling of our powerlessness takes over. This can manifest in anger, withdrawal and disconnection for you and your child. Judgement is a reaction that removes even more power from them, because it says, 'You're wrong, whatever you feel, and I am in charge.'

Use your experience, wisdom and compassion to take a bigger view of what is really going on. Not just the immediate behaviour – either yours or theirs – but what lies beneath it. Ask yourself: How am I responding? Why am I responding as I am?

To explore our feelings of judgement, we need to explore ourselves, our beliefs about our role and our own power. Ask yourself where your judgement has come from. Is it other people's judgement of what should be happening that is driving yours? Or is it a belief that you've held from your own childhood? Don't worry about whether it is right or wrong – you just need to identify it.

Emotions are physiologically driven, but if we can identify them, we don't have to act on them. How often have you gone along with what you feel, rather than challenging it? How often have you got angry, only to reflect after the point? The damage is done by your reaction in the moment, so if you can begin to reflect before you act, you'll be doing more good to build rapport and trust than you know.

When you're in the moment of judgement, try to draw upon your experience, not your emotion, and remember that the child in front of you is sharing their heart and soul through their actions.

Your feelings are born from experience. For example, you've learned that some families have dinner together and that it is 'better' than not having dinner together. And when that doesn't happen, you feel bad, or let down, or frustrated, and then your emotions kick in. You become angry. You feel sad. You act and make your feelings known. You feel triumphant. Or deflated. Whichever, it's likely that at no point have you considered why this is happening or how your child is feeling, because you 'know best'.

In these moments, make a conscious decision to pause the judgement. Look at any situation that causes you to engage your emotions as an opportunity for understanding. Why is your child hiding in their bedroom? If it's becoming an issue, look beyond your emotional response. You might not get the answers, but the simple act of acknowledging they are there and there is an issue opens up an acceptance that can lead to future connection.

Judgement of our child can be the only tool we feel we have to try to stop mental health decline and it comes from a sense of helplessness in ourselves: 'I'm the parent, I should be able to stop this.'

To a greater or lesser extent we might all use 'coping mechanisms' at times in our lives, whether alcohol, drugs, mindless scrolling or excessive busyness. We are all human. Suspending your judgement and seeing this time as an opportunity to explore your own beliefs may help. If that's not possible, just deciding that your judgements don't need to be shared out loud to your child, because they don't help, will be beneficial.

> Judgement can erode your child's sense of belief and self because it challenges the truth of the stories they know about themselves and their reactions begin to make those falsehoods real. Believe your child, their experience and their feelings.

Judgement doesn't help you or your child. You might feel powerful in that moment, but as a caring parent, watching your child's self-belief and self-esteem field the punches from your words is not a win. Judgement adds yet another thing our children have to fight. It isolates them from the person who they should be able to depend upon, without question. Your child needs you to care, not to judge. And even if you can't understand why, or don't recognise you're doing it, make the change and resist sharing everything you think and feel.

The 'Jenvy' Cycle

What is the difference between envy and jealousy? With envy, you want something but also want the person who has it to keep it too. With jealousy, you want it, and for the other person not to have it at all. When understanding why you can't have what you want is all mixed up, highly emotive and out of your control, you can find yourself flipping between a strange mix of both. It's called 'jenvy', and it's really normal when your child is mentally ill.

Social media is a constant source of potential hurt and irritation when your child is ill. Watching others' seemingly perfect lives can be painful and feed into our feelings of inadequacy and failure. We can easily forget that an image on social media is a carefully curated snapshot of a life, and simply long for it to be ours.

Questions can taunt you from the screen: Why can't we be that smiley, happy family on Facebook, enjoying each other's company, celebrating exam results, going out shopping? It might just be hearing about what your friends are up to, as they go about their 'normal' lives. It can help to tell yourself that your time will come.

In an attempt to spare you the same frustrations, pain, tears and tantrums as I went through, try these tips to deal with 'jenvy':

1. Acknowledge your emotion. Be clear about why you feel like that. Maybe you can't see a time when you will be able to go on holiday or your child will be able to leave the house. Maybe you're just plain angry. Whatever it is, open up to how you're really feeling. Your feelings will help release your internal pressure valve and help you move towards acceptance.

2. Allow yourself to grieve for the life you had before mental illness. Anything is possible after this experience, but letting go of the life you thought you and your child were going to lead is essential. Bid it a fond farewell if you can, or set it aside with kindness if it feels just too raw and painful at the

moment. Try to settle into this new routine. Find the pockets of joy wherever they might be.

3. Don't beat yourself up. Yes, we've all wanted something we haven't got and just because your child is ill and life is topsy-turvy, it doesn't stop you being human. Recognise your feelings, thank your mind for bringing up emotions you may need to address and don't give yourself a hard time.

4. Maybe there are some ways you can get a little of what you fancy. Can't go on holiday? Plan your ultimate trip on a Pinterest board and, when the time is right, you'll be ready to fly. Can't go out for a romantic meal with your partner? Take over the kitchen table and set it for two. Dim the lights, pour the wine and make the most of what you have. Is shopping too much for your child? Get your laptop and go online shopping together. It might not be perfect, but it's what works now.

5. Keep your eyes on the real prize. Long-haul trips, new trainers or school successes are all great, but the most important thing is the people in your world – your child, your family, you.

Dealing with Outside Pressure

One of the hardest things for us as parents of a child with a mental illness is trying to keep up with and field the expectations of the world around us. Some people feel they have a right to judge, and not just silently.

People feel they can query why your child isn't in school, why your child is wearing headphones and not talking, why your child isn't going to family events. Part of it, I believe, is curiosity and part of it is peer discovery. Whatever the reason, it is tiring to deal with, not to mention rarely any of their business.

The pressure we are surrounded by – to conform to the

stereotype of how a good life should be led – can become oppressive and damaging for you and for your child.

Many of my own experiences have shown me that the very structures we are led to believe will 'save' us and keep us on the right track can be irritants to our mental well-being and balance (such as school, eating three meals a day, etc.). Even simple daily acts aren't *simple* or possible when you're battling your mind.

Turning down the volume on these pressures can give you some space, and remove some of the noise about the future and your expectations of how you should be responding or reacting. It can allow you to focus on the job in hand – the really important work of getting your child stable and getting you all through.

Creating this mental space will enable you to regroup and to face each day with a sense of capability. If we take every day as it comes, on its own merits, without measuring it against other people's expectations, it makes it easier on us, and it makes it easier for our children.

If a child feels that they constantly have to perform, that you have expectations of them, that saying no is a weakness or defect, or if they have that Sunday night feeling every day of the week, how can we expect them to begin to heal? How can we expect them to begin to understand themselves if they are constantly fighting us, their illness, the norms and the expectations?

Our job as parents is to create a safe space where our children are supported, where they are believed, where they are nurtured and where they are loved. That safe space is not always on our terms; sometimes it's on their terms. Those best interests might not be what everybody else wants or expects; they might not be what the school says is the right thing or what your grandmother thinks they should be doing. Our role is to help them through this time, to become better at understanding their own needs, to support them and to validate them as the whole, wonderful human they are. It's OK to set pressure aside, for now or for the longer term. Give yourselves a break.

Your child needs you to look forward

I believe you must try to come to terms with your fear and fight as your child needs you to believe. Belief is hope on dark days, and sometimes it takes a leap of faith and a load of fortitude on your part to not look at the fragments of the life you knew and believe that this is your new forever. You may not be able to see the whole path ahead or know where you're going, but you can take one step forward with belief. You can tell your child, and yourself, that you believe that they will come through this, that they do have a future, and this will not impact on their ability to live a purposeful, happy life.

Keep in mind . . .

1. Feelings of fear, guilt, frustration, jealousy, envy and more are all normal. Identifying and acknowledging these human fears will help you understand what is happening to you and help you help your child.

2. It is natural to feel judgemental towards your child during this time; however, it is almost always counterproductive to you and your relationship with them.

3. You are not alone. There is a community of parents and healthcare professionals out there who know what you are experiencing and can help. Search 'Parenting Mental Health' on Facebook.

5

Understanding the Curve of Mental Illness

As the parent of a child with mental health problems, perhaps the most difficult thing to understand is the direction, duration and difficulty of the journey you now find yourself on. Is this going to be forever? When I see signs of change, does it mean the dark days are over? When can I begin to hope? It may be helpful to get a sense of the 'shape' of what your child is facing and get a sense of perspective on what they're going through. We are going to look at that now – what I call the 'curve' of mental illness.

Everyone's experience is unique

I'll be straight up with you. No one knows how long mental illness will last. We can try our hardest to help, we can take on board all of the professional advice, medication and therapies, and yet there is still no definitive prognosis that fits everyone – it's a highly personalised experience.

We hope it is a finite problem, yet it seems to work on an infinite timescale.

As the parent of a child with mental health problems, perhaps the most difficult thing to understand is the direction and duration of the journey you all now find yourselves on.

Watching your child's mental health change can create a sense of hopelessness that is difficult to appreciate and can make you feel defeated before you've even really begun. Is this going to be forever?

> 'The uncertainty of my son's mental health is so hard. It means I cannot look forward without fear or dread. Anyone passing the time of day inevitably talks about their child and I have that sick feeling, just waiting for them to ask me about M.'
>
> D, parent of 17-year-old

I created the Parenting Mental Health 'curve' as a way for us to gain some insight into the journey, and to understand where we have come from and what is likely to be ahead. It was based on our experiences as a family and has been validated by many other parents with a mentally ill child.

Recognising where your child is on the curve can give you peace of mind that there is a path out of the place you currently find yourself in, and bring you a sense of control. It can also enable you to recognise the needs of your child at each stage, as well as yourself. As you begin to understand the nature of the journey, you can steel yourself, stop petitioning the illness for respite and begin to gain a sense of control through understanding.

I see the curve as having six stages, each with different symptoms, each requiring specific strategies to deal with them. Each stage offers opportunities to understand what might be going on and how your behaviour may impact on the trajectory of the illness.

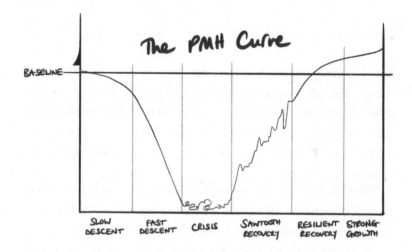

The PMH Curve

BASELINE

SLOW DESCENT | FAST DESCENT | CRISIS | SAWTOOTH RECOVERY | RESILIENT RECOVERY | STRONG GROWTH

The curve is different for everyone

It's important to say that this curve isn't a prescribed route – once you start it, it's not a given that you will go through all the stages. If your child is in the earlier stages of the journey, forget what is ahead and focus on where you are now. In each stage, you can support your child and slow down the 'descent' of your child's mental health issues. There are a number of ways we can 'bridge' the stages and help our child to move across, rather than through, all of the curve, including changing the way we communicate, the expectations and assumptions we make, and behaviours that build and encourage trust. Overall, the curve is there as a guide, to help you make some sense of what you might be seeing, and help you and your child to make a resilient recovery.

Baseline

The first thing to check is your child's 'baseline' mental health. This is not a definitive figure or something like BMI; it's where your child is at their most mentally well. This state is where they are exploring the world on their terms, and the things they learn about themselves and others aren't causing significant harm to them.

Your child's baseline mental health is made up of the level of resilience that your child generally possesses and uses to cope with life, how they respond when pressures are placed on them or taken away, and generally how balanced and happy they are. Factors in the baseline include an ability to maintain meaningful relationships, successfully process aggression or the negative behaviour of others, have a sense of personal pride in their appearance and values, and a desire to be productive, creative and independent, if appropriate. The baseline will be different for each child and there's no right or wrong. It's about seeing where they are at their best so you can see where they are now – up or down – from this position. This relies on your knowledge of the child and is a measure that really only you and those your child trusts can perceive.

Think of a time when they were most 'themselves', when external factors weren't creating tension or changes in their behaviour. Have they always been emotional? Angry? Resilient? Quiet? How far away from that are they now? Just 'note' this to yourself.

Stage One: Slow Descent

This is the beginning of the curve, and most of the time this stage goes unnoticed. We often reason this time away and attribute it to 'teenage tantrums' or our child displaying unreasonable behaviour. We're busy and, though it's not something to be proud of, it can feel like a big pain in the backside to confront these behaviours in our children.

Because stage one only very slowly gets more serious, your child may be in this stage for years and it can be hard to spot. They may adjust their behaviour and their expectations of themselves to shield themselves from the internal fallout of declining mental health. They may detach from you and the closeness you have felt because they don't want to confront the feelings or the triggers that are challenging their mental health. Feelings around their self-esteem and body image can lead them to isolate themselves more, physically and emotionally, and leave some of their emotions and beliefs unchallenged and unseen.

Children can fall into this 'slow descent' through a range of situations. Maybe they have suffered a bereavement, but haven't been able to process it. School pressures may feel overwhelming, but they don't feel they can ask for help. Perhaps they are being bullied or are part of a toxic relationship. Sometimes it is from an event – possibly they've recovered from another illness or have suffered a trauma. If this hasn't been acknowledged or validated, or they've been rushed to overcome or ignore their feelings, it can lead to the start of a decline in their mental health. Maybe they are finding their changing body, sexuality or opinions difficult to reconcile with the rest of their world.

Your child's self-esteem will be beginning to fall, along with their belief in their ability to effect change in their lives. Their separation from friends and family may begin, and they may change their interests, start to hang out with new friends or change their routines in an attempt to gain some control.

As we know, the teenage years are downright difficult, with hormonal shifts, friendship changes, academic pressure and the urgency to find out who they are as people. It can be hard to see the difference between universal teenage challenges and when we should be worrying about something deeper and potentially life-changing. Sometimes it's only with the benefit of hindsight that we can see the small signs that show this is something to be monitored. I only saw in reverse that Issy was slipping. I was blindly thinking I could love away issues that came up, and didn't stop – or couldn't bring myself – to ask if this was something that needed deeper consideration. I saw that Issy's self-esteem was falling; she was less able to see the beauty in things that used to bring her joy; she was more tired than usual. Any one of these might ebb and flow due to external factors like school and friendship changes, but when there is more than one, it's a possibility that your child is finding their mental health a challenge to manage.

Stage Two: Fast Descent

As the effects of the slow descent gather pace, you may find yourself becoming aware that this isn't *just* teenage hormones or a phase, and something really isn't right. You are aware that your child's behaviour is not 'normal' and signs of depression or anxiety will become more obvious and clear. You'll see rapid and/or radical changes, as your child tries to assert control over their life.

Your child may have begun to seek solace in excessive gaming, vaping, drug-taking or other escapes, refuse school on occasion, get into trouble with teachers or police, adversely change their eating habits, separate themselves from their peer group or appear to be very emotional. Their sleep pattern may have changed and any interaction can turn into a fight where they are unable to communicate how they feel. They may constantly question your authority at this point and seem to be 'lost' or 'distant'. They will be using their changing behaviours to find ways to effect change over their life and, if appropriate, the reasons behind their poor mental health. Over time, as this stage gets more acute, they may start making plans for self-harm or suicide.

> 'At this stage, everything was getting worse and there was disconnect between my own happiness and what I felt I could do to change it. I had tried so hard to change things, but I just couldn't. It felt like things would always be the same, so I stopped trying. I decided that I would just exist, because nothing mattered anymore. And then when that seemed pointless, I found myself spiralling deeper and deeper.'
>
> Issy

In the fast descent stage, your child's mental health is an issue, but it's likely it's not *the* issue for you. You'll be trying to mitigate the fallout with school, family and others they interact with. You may be angry at them for their changing behaviours and find it hard to empathise. You may still not be aware of the extent of their descent and not see what's really going on. Or you may be like me, and still kid yourself you can love this away. This stage is critical in defining whether your child will end up in crisis and it offers a chance to bridge across the most difficult times and take their mental health seriously.

Stage Three: Crisis

This is the stage we obviously want to avoid. None of us wants a child in crisis. Your child will feel that there is little hope for change when they are in crisis. Their decision-making at this stage may make them appear uncommunicative and aggressive. They will have come to some personal conclusions about their life, its meaning, their situation, your views, opinions of them and what you deem important, plus their future prospects. They will have decided that more radical behaviour is required for them to rid themselves of the suffering and isolation they are feeling. They may be consistently aggressive towards themselves and/or authority figures and feel any and all activity is meaningless. They may punch walls or damage furniture. They will be at a point where they feel they need to escape the situation they are in and may take drastic action – attempt suicide, run away, repeatedly or severely self-harm, or slip into a self-destructive torpor. They may not be sleeping, or sleeping excessively; they may be using food or drugs as a form of control; they may not be able to leave the house or engage with friends or family; they may give up washing and taking care of themselves. You may wonder where your child has gone and if they'll ever be back.

Crisis makes your child's mental health *the* issue, not *an* issue. It forces someone – you, your child or another interested party – to confront and address what is going on. It changes everything and gives you the chance to choose your child and their mental health. Crisis questioned me and my parenting, and presented me with an unwanted but urgent opportunity to decide if I was going to fight for the status quo or embrace what was really going on and change the way I supported Issy, for her benefit. Crisis is probably one of the most difficult and challenging times that you will encounter in your life.

Crisis is an indeterminate period of sustained fear, which in itself takes a great toll on you, as you fear so much for your child. It demands your attention, respect and action. It insists that you sign up to a new set of rules. It is the ultimate fight – for your child's health and future self.

Stage Four: Sawtooth Recovery

Coming out of crisis is a very bumpy road. You might start to see the glimmers of hope – a smile, an agreement to shower, perhaps less tension around treatment. Good days may be followed by bad ones, but they do exist.

As a few good days string together you (and sometimes your child) may believe the worst is over, the future is now bright and the good times are now certain.

As crisis responses recede, it's easy to rush into recovery, forcing progress and expecting to pick up on life where you left it. 'Sawtooth' recovery is an opportunity to reassess the life you had against the life you need.

We can fall back into pre-mental illness patterns of behaviour quickly as we rush to return to the life we had before everything changed, loading expectation and assumptions on our child. This can pressure them at a time where they are taking tentative steps towards recovery. It takes a lot of energy and courage to try something new when you're in a mental health crisis, and so what may appear like a win for you will undoubtedly have taken a toll on them, leading to a drop after a high. This is really normal and to be expected.

This is the time to gently help your child to equip themselves with the tools and techniques to recognise the steps backwards. If sawtooth recovery were a dance, it would be a cha-cha-cha danced by a novice; two steps forward, four steps left, a step backwards and a tangle of feet. It is not linear. And it can be messy and frustrating.

Whatever happiness you've seen, there will be bad days and usually many of them. Sliding back into crisis is a possibility, particularly if the expectation to recover is overwhelming or the fundamental reasons behind the mental illness have not been adequately addressed. Coming out of crisis and beginning to rebuild yourself is painstaking work and it takes commitment, space and time.

> Every child's recovery is unique to them. And it is necessary to recognise there will still be bad days and to accept them as part of the curve, and as part of life. By expecting and accepting the bad days you can lessen their impact on you and your child.

Stage Five: Resilient Recovery

The time, techniques and connection that have brought you and your child out of crisis into sawtooth recovery can now start to strengthen your child. In stage five you will begin to experience more good days than bad, and new behaviours and attitudes are making you and your child believe in the progress being made. You can now move into the 'resilient recovery' phase, a time to test and trial new experiences and challenges.

In this stage you can start to introduce and encourage the use of psychological techniques and behavioural changes that can help your child prevent themselves from sliding backwards. You can help them anticipate the stressors that may have caused or accelerated their decline in the first place and enable them to understand themselves better.

Part of being resilient is about protecting ourselves from potential triggers, and this stage of the curve is a delicate balance of push and pull where you are directed by your child's curiosity and encourage them to try to believe in themselves, with your support.

Resilient recovery is not about perfection. All recovery is a practice and a process. We all try to test experiences and see what works and what doesn't. We tweak and try again.

Recovery in your child works in the same way. Maybe they need to rethink some of their choices, to maintain their mental well-being. Maybe you do too.

Find your support team

I always advocate finding other people who are experiencing the same challenges as you (see page 64). Their experiences can become guiding lights in the depths of descent and illuminate the potential for change for recovery. If they're further along the curve, they can often share that what you feel are desperate setbacks are natural and overcomeable. That you are making progress, even if it seems slower than a snail's pace. A shared experience gives us impetus and perspective to take action, however counter-intuitive and wrong it feels to embrace something as distasteful as mental illness. Not going through it alone gives us the strength that this battle so efficiently steals from us.

Stage Six: Strong Growth

This is the stage where you find yourself at baseline mental health (see page 68) and ready to go beyond it. The experience of mental illness can now be owned and somewhat, if not fully, understood by you and your child. When you get to the strong growth phase, you and your child will understand yourselves and each other better. The behaviour, attitude and lifestyle changes that have brought them through the curve can now be used to improve their mental health further. This journey can make you and your child mentally stronger, mentally happier and far more self-aware and resilient.

This is a stage that we hope will last for the rest of your child's life, where they can accept who they are and can hopefully avoid repeated events of depression or anxiety; a stage where they can actively create a happy, purposeful life on their terms.

Our mental health is a continuum. Of course, setbacks and disappointments will still happen, but if you reflect on the experiences and skills you and your child have accumulated throughout the curve, you can see them for what they are: challenges to be overcome, rather than a guarantee of mental health decline.

Bridging the curve

It can be frustrating to see the rollercoaster shape of the curve. It can feel like it will be never-ending and there's no hope of control, but there is always hope. If you see that your child is slipping down the curve, you don't have to watch them slip into crisis. There are things you can do to help them 'bridge' a potential crisis and move towards better mental health.

'Bridging' is avoiding or reducing the impact of the early stages of the curve by 'partnering' your child, which we'll look at in the next two chapters. By acknowledging the situation you are in, changing your behaviour towards your child, providing support for your child to see a way out of their situation and addressing some of the external triggers to your child's mental health decline, you can help to bridge the stages before further decline. You will find ideas and strategies to do this throughout this book. There is always hope.

Our Experience of the Curve

Changing behaviour at any point in life takes determination and courage. It took me a while to grasp how my behaviour was impacting on Issy's illness; it didn't happen upon me one day. Coming to terms with what we were facing, what Issy's reality was, what my part was in this sorry affair, all took time and reflection and compassion, and that continued through every stage of the curve. As a parent you experience your own 'curve' of this experience. Accepting where we were was hard, because I had to override the feature in my parental operating system where I was often compelled to fix, fix, fix, with all the best intentions. Again, time and compassion helped me come to terms with this and that this wasn't my illness to control.

I didn't realise it at the beginning, but this experience was the start of a new and compassionate approach to Issy and to my life. A feeling that grew within me rapidly was a sense that Issy was being challenged and changed by this experience (as were we as parents) and, however and whenever we got through, there would be changes. We wouldn't all be in the same place. In order to reduce the friction, I had to engage more patience, empathy and tolerance. And this approach supported us all as we encouraged Issy to consider curiosity, on her terms and timescale, and we began to build a shared vision of recovery that we tried and refined as we all emerged from crisis.

It took time for me to see the benefits of bridging the gaps by changing my behaviour. How could these small changes in how I responded really impact on Issy's mental health? But they did, and for every day we shielded her from the expectations to race back to life, created space for her and held it open whether she wanted it or not, we moved an imperceptible space towards deeper understanding and something that felt elusive at times – recovery.

Keep in mind . . .

1. Understanding what the journey may look like helps you frame your behaviour in a positive way.
2. You can bridge the worst parts of the journey if you recognise and act quickly.
3. You can 'beat' the baseline – your child (and you!) can come through this with strength and resilience they didn't have before.

6

Partnering, not Parenting

Partnering is about walking beside your child, recognising that this journey is theirs and that, while you have a role to play in it, it is not yours to control.

Reflecting on my parenting style pre-2015, I'd say I was always a 'collaborative' parent. Yes, I made decisions, but I took my children's views into account. I was unconsciously focused on finding the best way forward for my children, within the confines of my own expectations and upbringing and those of society. Until Issy became mentally ill.

Waking up to the reality of a world where my daughter no longer wanted to live was a process and it took quite some time. I went into 'fix' mode. I tried to control the small things I could; tried to simplify the complexity of what was going on into a set of routines that would just get us through that day. I tried to just get her to school, to eat dinner with us, to talk more, so this whole horrible time would vanish as quickly as it had seemed to arrive. My concern and care manifested in behaviours that really didn't convey to Issy the depth of love, and fear, I held for her. They also didn't offer the kind of calm, measured stability she needed.

As parents, we didn't recognise what was going on, and we didn't know what to do for the best. When we tried to force change with Issy, take decisions on her behalf or approach the circumstances with a mix of authority and bluster, our best intentions made things worse and Issy drifted further away from us.

I soon came to see that, however much I continued, my behaviour really wasn't helping. Something had to change. As mental illness had set up shop in our daughter's mind and wasn't going anywhere, I realised that I couldn't 'change' Issy or demand anything of her illness. It was not our job to fix her. It had become difficult and frustrating to see that we were becoming a part of the problem, because we just wanted to help, and I know it was completely isolating and distressing for her.

School and showers and sleep were simply not possible for her during the early days; they weren't going to fix the underlying issues, and they were pushing her further away from wellness. Telling somebody who can't do these things that they must only has one outcome, and that is to detach them from you. There had to be another way.

A New Approach to 'Parenting'

I began to grasp that Issy needed to be heard and supported by us if she was going to have any kind of hope of recovery. Every time we loaded her with pre-mental illness expectation, she believed less that we understood her and needed to hide away to tend to her wounds, alone. Every time we tried, with the best of intentions, to force or cajole or (embarrassingly) blackmail her into change, we all lost.

I wasn't 'in charge' of her illness or her recovery. I was a steward of it and needed to be an advocate for her needs. I needed to respond to her, not react to what the rest of the world expected or I hoped for. I needed to stop trying to fix it and allow her to process it. We had to find a way to work together, and I call this new way of parenting 'partnering'.

Think of a time when you've been treated like a child, whether by a boss, a friend or your own parents, and remember how disempowering and disconnecting it feels. 'Partnering' gives you an opportunity to create an equality between child and parent that fosters positive, meaningful connection and understanding out of a very challenging situation.

With 'partnering', you can create a space that allows your child to speak openly to you about what they are going through, without fear of judgement, anger or disappointment.

If your child finds themselves at the point where they want to harm themselves or attempt to end their own life, where do they go? If you're a 'Do as I say' parent it is unlikely that they'll come to you because they may assume you will judge or won't understand. By partnering your child, you can be the accepting, safe haven as your child begins to trust that your reaction won't diminish their pain, and their needs will be heard and respected. In time, you can build a new shared language that connects you and reminds you both that there is common respect and support.

How many conversations did you not have as a child because you feared your parents' response? How much did you have to process and carry alone because you couldn't share what was going on? Partnering is about opening up the potential for connection. It is a shift in the means of communication and understanding between you and your child. At a time when they need compassion, empathy and understanding more than ever, let's aim to not be just another person who doesn't get them, who doesn't understand, who they can't trust or rely on.

Partnering is about equality in power, it's about respect and it is about compassion for another person. Partnering says, 'I am not trying to fix you, I am here to support you. I understand that you're not in charge of all your behaviours or responses because you are struggling with trauma, pain, distress, disconnection, or any personal mix of these.' It is about acknowledging the other person's situation and their right to feel how they feel, rather than looking at them as a child to be told what to do.

I found partnering to be the simplest and most effective way to ensure I gave Issy the best support I could. It helped her to recover and become a strong, resilient, happy, well young woman. And many other parents in the Parenting Mental Health community have changed their relationships with their children and emerged from mental illness stronger and closer than before. You'll hear from one of them later in this chapter.

Managing other people's ideas

You may be told by friends, family, schools and medical professionals that you need to enforce rules when your child is ill. You'll be questioned in that depressingly patronising and isolating way about why your child isn't doing the 'normal' things that society expects. And you may find yourself enforcing rules that you know in your heart of hearts won't work, while holding on to the hope that somehow they will this time.

If your child has a mental illness, they are unlikely to be being obstructive for the sake of it. They are likely to be spending all their energy and effort on getting through each day without being consumed by what is going on in their minds. They are likely to be unable to deal with the events and activities that you are trying to force them into. And at this time, they need connection more than ever.

The Three Stages of Partnering

When the tactics and strategies of our usual day-to-day parenting aren't helping (or may be actively harming) our child's mental health, partnering may help. My partnering experiences with Issy took me through three stages:

1. Step down
2. Stand beside
3. Travel together

I share what these mean below, and how you may be able to adjust the way you approach your child and their needs as you go forward.

Stage 1: Step down

'Stepping down' is the first move in partnering, and it's probably the bravest. Stepping down shifts our role as a parent away from being the authority (the one in charge who knows how to cope and is able to fix things) to one where we provide a nurturing and accepting space for our child. This space will allow your child to feel what they're feeling and explore what they need without our expectations of what they should do, be or feel.

Stepping down means letting go of expectations and assumptions. You may need to accept that you can't fix the situation, but that you can influence it.

Changing your behaviour is not a parenting failure and stepping down isn't a denial of your responsibilities. Stepping away from knowing it all and having to have all the answers doesn't leave our children to run feral or allow mental illness to set in. See this as an opportunity for deeper connection, when connection was starting to feel unobtainable.

Stepping down can feel counterproductive, because we're hardwired as parents to defend and protect our offspring. But it is definitely not about caring less about your child or endangering them in some way. This is about giving yourself permission to try something different, to see yourself as a part of the change needed, not the person in control of the outcome.

Stepping down releases you from the presumptions of a world that doesn't live with your child or understand their mental illness. It offers your child the acceptance and support that means so much when battling mental illness.

Stepping down is about being responsible, considered and conscious around your child's needs. It's about being in a place where you can build an approach that works for your family; one that recognises and respects your child's right to a voice if they are going to recover resiliently. It is a powerful way of removing the barriers to understanding so you can genuinely express your support for your child, share in their experience and build an unbreakable bond.

We can 'step down' by sharing how we've changed our behaviour, by showing we're on their side in what we say and how we behave. We can reinforce it through consistency and honesty. Pretending to change our approach, only to revert to 'I know best' when they share a feeling or desire that we don't want to entertain or encourage, damages any progress we may have made. In that case, the process of stepping down may have to begin again in part or in its entirety. Don't worry – we all do it, but by knowing about its potential for disconnection in advance, we can look out for where this change feels difficult and begin to examine our reactions before they pop out and trash all the hard-won connection we've been building.

Stage 2: Stand beside

As we set aside the belief that we hold the answers to and authority over our child's mental illness, we can start to really support them with a different approach – standing beside them. And as we stand beside them, shoulder to shoulder, without judgement, they can begin to explore what their mental health needs really are and make sense of what is really going on and how it might improve.

Standing beside your child gives you a new perspective and a shared outlook; it might not be one that you like, want or approve of, but if you can respect your child's needs, both practically and to be heard and validated, you can begin to take steps in a shared direction towards recovery.

To do this, we need to open up a new space where our child is accepted for all they are, whether we agree with it or not, and where they have agency and opportunity over how their illness is dealt with. Holding this space, without judgement or 'helpful' interjection on how we think this might be fixed, validates their emotions and the reality they hold.

If you are struggling to make sense of their reality, that's OK. Showing that you believe in the pain they're enduring and will act to defend their needs is a generous and compassionate gift. Changing your perspective to stand beside them offers them control at a time when they have little. This, coupled with the belief from you – someone who is perceived by them to hold power over them – gives them permission and validation that what they're feeling is their right. In time, this opens up a safe space where they can share their feelings with you and inform your shared perspective.

Standing beside Issy enabled her to believe that she had the authority and power to change the things that were causing her mental distress. She didn't have to change them all by herself (that was a team effort), but she could use her voice to share what was hurting and what was working.

As we stand beside our child, the important work of building trust can begin. This takes time and effort. If we've leaned heavily on 'Do as I say' up until now, we should expect to have to prove that we've stepped down from being the all-knowing authority and that our child can really rely on us to respect what they feel, whatever they disclose.

Being a shield for our child also helps to build trust and offers them a safe place where they can begin to process what they're feeling without the weight of our judgements or expectations. For example, when Issy couldn't go to school, I became her voice, shield and advocate. I was challenged by professionals and officials on why she wasn't attending school or, once we had removed her from school, why she wasn't engaging with home education. Issy and I had agreed that school wasn't possible and it was exacerbating her mental health issues, so I stood our ground, ensuring she knew that I understood that she couldn't go and that I would represent her needs without apology. I didn't need to know why or when she would go back to school. I trusted that she couldn't and wanted her to have the emotional freedom to get better.

Making a commitment to stand beside your child helps you to take it seriously, especially when things are hard. Being honest, with yourself and them, when you struggle to let go of the tendencies to fix things helps your child to stop feeling like any control or voice they have is being taken away. This is a process and a practice, and it's important to share that you may struggle to find your feet with this new way of being.

When your child begins to see that you are standing beside them wholeheartedly and accepting them for all they are, despite their mental illness and how you think or wish things would be, magical connections can happen. You can begin to 'travel together' through this time.

'My style of parenting had always been a mixture of lots of love, peppered with "Do as you are told" and "Mum knows best". This worked for my family until my daughter struggled with her mental health at the age of 15 where we faced suicide attempts and self-harm. All of a sudden there were no quick fixes and my usual methods of parenting were not working. She was anxious and depressed and I felt guilt. I lost confidence and I was floundering. In my eyes I had failed as a parent. When I started partnering I did not expect how empowering it would be.

'I learned so much about myself and how, no matter what mistakes I had made in the past, by just tweaking my behaviours now I could make such a difference to my child's recovery. Each week I became calmer and braver as I applied what I was learning. I learned I couldn't fix my child but I could walk alongside her and be her shield and her voice. As a result, our relationship grew stronger, I was able to listen not to respond, but to understand. I became a great role model to my child by taking self-care seriously and showing I valued myself. During a recent setback for my daughter, I felt so calm – I had the tools and faith in the lessons I'd learned to give her space, understanding and encouragement. I was able to show faith in her decisions and she found her voice. It was music to my ears to hear her say she notices the difference in my approach. She says I am calmer and thanks me for listening and allowing her to own her power and to decide what she's ready for.'

J, parent of 17-year-old

Stage 3: Travel together

Travelling together puts us on a path of exploration with our child, where they can begin to delve into what works for them and trust themselves and their choices.

There will be detours, dead ends and days when you wonder where this will lead. Agreeing together to start to explore and allowing them to lead with their interests and needs will yield some unusual and unexpected results. With Issy, gaming was the direction she took and we travelled with her, metaphorically and literally.

Some of the results you'll get won't be what either of you want, and there will be challenges. Your child will be fighting their mind and trying to get a foothold so they can create a sense of stability from where they can begin to heal and recover. But the more you trust in them, and show you are there to co-create and support their recovery, not own it, the more they will too. And all sorts of open conversations, choices and change will begin to come.

This is not the time to worry about short-term direction or destination. This is a time to encourage movement and change, led by them, wherever that may lead you. You will need to put down your questions about when they are coming off their medication or how they see their future, and allow them to work on recovering resiliently.

This stage isn't linear – it will zig and zag and, just as you think you understand where you are, it can take you somewhere else. Issy found a purpose and confidence through gaming and the associated activities of digital art commissions, coaching a team, making cosplay and streaming. We enjoyed seeing her explore and take what she needed from it, and when it led to her wanting to go back into education, she followed a path that none of us had ever considered.

No one can accurately say how long it will take before you see movement or where it will take you. Issy and I have continued to travel together, with me as her trusted companion as she navigates life after mental illness.

This might all be very uncomfortable for you at times. As we see glimmers of change, we might want to go straight in and fix things, instead of allowing our child to explore and grow on their terms. Keeping our communication open and our intent positive can help us to understand the rationale behind the sometimes unexplainable routes our children might take.

But it's not forever. We should enjoy the victories, without judgement and with a sense of curiosity in what our children can discover about themselves as they battle their brains and fight for wellness. It's a time to really appreciate the differences you're seeing, especially when you begin to notice the glimmers of hope that change is on its way.

As we see our child emerging, we can want to use our experience to direct and trim any unnecessary pain or hurt for our child. But this isn't about perfection, it's about progress.

There is no wrong route here, just the ultimate goal of your child being happy and healthy. They might not be following the traditional path or the one you had hoped for, but this isn't yours to define. It's an opportunity for them to uncover and understand deeply what they need, what they want – in this moment and maybe beyond – and to begin to feel good about themselves again.

Celebrate the small wins

During the three stages of partnering, take time to observe and celebrate the small wins (that might be huge for you!) – a walk outside together, a decision to start a course or, in Issy's case, a choice to sell her art at a fair. The walk outside doesn't mean they're now planning an expedition, nor does the course mean they will now take this direction as a career. Selling prints at a fair was one small element in Issy's exploration of her needs and wants, and a step towards rebuilding her confidence and self-belief. Focus on the joy of the activity, rather than where it might lead or what it might mean. Embrace the uncertainty and relish those wins, today. They may lead somewhere, they may not. Either way it's fine. It's better to travel together, than to arrive. There is hope.

A pot of positives

Every New Year's Eve, we sit down and review the year that's gone and set our goals and intentions for the year ahead. In 2016, we added the 'pot of positives' into the proceedings and, as they spilled out and on to the kitchen table, it was a very real reminder that so much had happened over the past 18 months. Those folded pieces of paper represented huge change for us; a reminder that nothing lasts forever, good or bad. Unfolding each one with anticipation gave us a huge sense of the transformation we'd all been through.

This was our way of recognising and remembering those small wins so that we could see the shifts on dark days. You might like to try it too:

1. Find a jar that you like. We used a simple Kilner jar.
2. Each time you notice a win, make a note of the date and what happened on a scrap of paper. They might be small things, like a day without crying, an attempt to go to school, time spent together laughing. You might like to use glitter pens for any big moments, like eating dinner together or attempting schoolwork.
3. You might not have something to add every day, and that's normal.
4. You might need to dip into the pot for a boost now and then, or you may choose a special day to open it up. You might like to put them in date order and, as you read through them, you can be reminded of how far you have all come.

Keep in mind . . .

1. Partnering is a new approach to parenting that removes the judgement and authority, but not the responsibility, to give your child agency and safety at a time when they feel they have little.
2. Stepping down from a place of ultimate authority opens up potential for trust and connection, which, at times, can be hard to find.
3. Standing beside your child can go against your expectations, but this is about creating a safe space for your child to explore their illness and consider recovery.
4. Travelling together is all about exploration of what life can look like after mental illness. Be open and curious and you may be surprised at what kind of future you can create together.

7

Practical Partnering

As parents, we have a unique opportunity to use our skills, love and experience to really make a difference to our child when they are mentally ill.

When you're in the thick of it, identifying the behaviours that might not support your child or validate their feelings is hard. Seeing what you're doing wrong requires a level of awareness that you might not feel is where your energy is best placed. In this chapter, we'll go through some of the ways that can help you to step down, stand beside your child and travel together.

It's not easy as a parent to face what is really going on or what our part is in that reality. We tell ourselves convenient stories (I know I did) as a way to cope and deal with experiences and feelings we might not enjoy or expect to experience. I doubt any of us dreamed of a time when our beautiful child struggled to go to school or needed medication for depression.

But before we can change anything, we have to know the real shape of what we're facing. I had my head in the sand for a good 18 months and I pretended 'I'd got this' as Issy's mental health declined. Nothing changed for the better while I ignored it. Acknowledgement took me from a safe and familiar point of denial, and encouraged me to bravely explore how I could support positive change by confronting the truth of what was going on and then stepping down from a place of absolute authority and standing beside Issy as her 'partner'.

The purpose of a child is not to make us feel complete or to serve our own 'needs'. Partnering is a reminder that the role that you have to play in your child's life is a privilege. It is improved when you build rapport based around respect and you approach your child as an equal human being, rather than something for you to manage, oversee or own.

> First of all, please don't beat yourself up about anything you discover as you reflect on your parenting. I've done enough berating for both of us. Please be really gentle with yourself and engage the kind of super-kindness and understanding that your best friend would offer you.

Start with Acknowledgement

Acknowledgement is an opportunity to see what is going on *now* with your child's mental health. Today, right now, is your chance to come to terms with where you are as a family, so you can see your current role and how you might change that to help influence a new outcome.

This is not a time to kick yourself; it's a learning opportunity, a chance to understand more about what is going on so you can help your child, your family and yourself through. It's also about understanding your child's facts and what's real for *them*, and then acknowledging the gaps. It's about challenging your perceptions of what's going on versus what's *really* going on. And it's about acknowledging the triggers and the ways you got to a place of distress, but not necessarily the reasons why.

No judgement.

We would all like to just pretend nothing is happening. Why can't we just carry on regardless? Well, we can, but, as I found out, it doesn't really help our child when we overlook the truth of their struggle or how we can influence it. It is invalidating and isolating for us and for them, both in the short term and in how they perceive themselves when we negate their feelings and their truth. A lack of acknowledgement can lead us to become overcritical, of ourselves and others, and can lead to disconnection with our child, family and ourselves.

So, how do we approach acknowledgment? There were five areas that I explored:

1. Your child's mental health

What is actually happening with your child? What has changed? What behaviours have begun and why? If a long-lost auntie from Outer Mongolia visited, what would she see that was unusual, in need of investigation or shouting 'Help me!'? What are the facts of the challenge you're facing?

For us, Issy not wanting to go to school was a red flag. So was her sleeping more, not engaging with the things she loved and crying every day. Don't be like me! It's not pleasant to see what's sad or desperate in our child, but acknowledge that there is an issue and what that looks like for your child.

So where do you start? You might have a feeling, a sense that things are not right and not the same, or it may be apparent through your child's words and actions. You may be feeling the impacts of what's really going on – your own stress levels may be high, your patience wearing thin and your energy levels taking a hit.

In your child, you might be seeing grades slipping or them losing interest or patience with something they once loved. Maybe their sleep pattern has shifted or they've stopped eating as much. Maybe you're seeing violent outbursts or they are crying more often. Perhaps they are more loving than before and need constant reassurance. Or a number of these things when you come to think of it.

Grab a notebook (one you can keep somewhere private) and make a list of the behaviours that you're seeing. If you can't put your finger on what has changed, write down what is frustrating you and see if this is because of a behaviour change in them. You're making this list for three reasons. Firstly, writing things down makes them more real and will help you to acknowledge what your child is going through. If you ever need a reminder that your child's mental health is in decline, this is it. Secondly, it will help you communicate with professionals. Thirdly, it's a benchmark. Things will change. They may get worse, but, in most cases, they will get better too. This is your way of seeing when those changes happen.

What is 'normal' teenage behaviour?

One of the most frequent questions I get asked is what is normal teenage behaviour and what is mental illness? How can a parent tell the difference? For me, any behaviour that you are questioning as the person who lives with your child every day deserves to be examined. Some examples of the kinds of behavioural changes that may indicate mental health issues include:

- Not wanting to spend time with friends or family and withdrawing socially.
- Refusal to attend school.
- Refusal to go to activities they previously enjoyed.
- Changes in sleep patterns (sleeping at strange times of the day, not being able to get to sleep, staying awake all night, not wanting to sleep alone, suddenly sleeping all the time).

- Changes in appetite (not eating, eating too much, only eating one type of food, eating too much sugar).
- Sudden changes in energy levels (feeling lethargic or feeling compelled to be busy, for example over-exercising or excessive cleaning).
- An increased focus on the familiar, needing more routine.
- Lack of interest in things that used to bring joy.
- Repeated acts of impatience, rudeness, anger and crying.
- Isolating themselves.
- Reckless behaviour.

2. Your behaviour and its impacts

Acknowledging that our own behaviour can and (likely) does have an impact on our child is a great starting point for deeper understanding and connection. And it's a tough one, I know! It's hard to reflect upon ourselves and our behaviour and see that, even though we come from a place of love, our intentions might get lost in translation and we can send the wrong messages.

Many of us are working to the timetable of society and, over time, we can become immune to the changes and challenges in ourselves and our child. We can find ourselves *being*, but not feeling. Responding, but not really considering. So, reflecting on what's really going on might feel a challenge or an indulgence.

Firstly, can you acknowledge that your parenting may be having an impact on your child, their mental health, how deeply they will deteriorate and how quickly they can get better? This is not a blame game. We love as well as we can at the time.

Ask yourself the following questions:

- Can you see that the way you speak to your child can impact on their mental health?
- Can you reflect on the impact of your reactions?
- How does your behaviour make your child feel?

Acknowledging the general tone of our behaviour and how we respond in certain situations can lead to a deep understanding of how things might escalate or be misconstrued by others. Are you transmitting from Planet Love, only for it to come across as nagging, uncompassionate or oblivious to your child's pain? Can you put yourself in your child's shoes and try to unpick their reaction?

And are you open to challenging the learned behaviours that you have been gifted by your own experiences? It's an interesting switch in the partnering process. Many of the parents I speak with are racked with guilt once they've acknowledged that their child's mental health is in decline. But it's also common for parents to be unable to see that they not only have a part to play, but also the *power to effect change*.

This is not a blame game

Once you've acknowledged you have a part to play in this, today and over time, ask yourself how your responses and reactions, expectations and routines are facilitating or exacerbating your child's mental health struggles. Remember: no blame. We're identifying these so we can examine and change them if necessary, not beat ourselves up about the kind of parents we are.

LOOKING AT OURSELVES IN THE MIRROR

The way we conduct ourselves is an unspoken blueprint for our children to follow. If we don't know how we behave, we can't change anything.

What are you doing that is facilitating poor mental health? Are you on your child's side? Do you show that, or are you exhausted and fire-fighting the whole time, with little presence or patience? What impact is that having?

Give yourself some time to reflect on where you're at. The point of acknowledgement is to be honest with yourself, to open your eyes to what's really going on, so you can begin to move to acceptance. Look beyond your fixation on the future you have planned. That might be acknowledging some hard truths; that your child won't make it to college next week or next term. (And that that's OK.) That your need for certainty isn't serving your child; that they can't meet your expectations, due to their mental health.

Our goal as a parent is to help our child become fully themselves and be able to unleash their unique gifts and energy on the world. Our role is to support them as they work towards becoming a resilient, happy, balanced human being capable of love and compassion. Notice there's no mention of exams, awards, sporting prizes, etc. And there's certainly no mention of building a compliant person who exists to serve your needs as a parent.

3. Your power to affect change in your life

Parents have such an important role in supporting children through their mental health challenges and into a resilient recovery. I believe as a parent we have the power to effect change in our family's lives, and so often we don't believe it. Now is the time to acknowledge that you have power! Not power to control, but to nurture, support and influence how you and your family respond to and recover from this.

4. Your strengths and needs

Acknowledging our strengths and what our needs are is really important if we're going to be at our most helpful and supportive. Being a parent tends to place us right at the back of the queue. But acknowledging your strengths and needs will help to get you through this. Consider your strengths – here are some that you might recognise in yourself:

- resilience
- patience
- optimism
- tenacity
- compassion
- commitment
- persistence
- tact
- thoughtfulness
- tolerance

Take time now to think about your 'needs' too. You might need to be kind to yourself. You may need support and connection. Put aside time to recharge your batteries and, when they begin to drain, prioritise this to help you be a better parent. Self-care can feel empty and pointless when your mind is whirring – a distraction from the urgent work of caring and surviving – but it's worth reframing it for your child's sake, and your own. When we take care of ourselves, we reduce the levels of dependency on our relationship with our child. Taking care of a child with a mental illness can lead us to lose our sense of self as the lines of experience blur and we become focused on and defined by their diagnosis, treatment and progress. Self-care allows us to rely on our own reserves to feel at peace, rather than our moods being influenced by our child's. When we're rested, calmer and have the perspective that immersion, escape or connection with things or people outside of our child offers, we become less dependent on the state of our child's health to determine our own levels of well-being. Self-care takes the obligation out of your relationship so you can give responsively and compassionately, while giving your child the freedom to explore their illness and themselves. Self-care takes away the worry of the impact of being honest about their feelings on your well-being and stops them feeling responsible for your happiness and approval. Without a doubt, self-care helps you, and your child. (See Chapter 9 for more on self-care.)

If you find this hard, I get it. I did too. Try to think of yourself as the blueprint for your child. They follow your behaviours, how you show you value yourself and how patient and non-judgemental you are to yourself. Judging ourselves doesn't help us and it doesn't help them either. Being compassionate and kind to ourselves is so important, especially when it comes to changing our behaviours. Acknowledge your needs and that they are valid and a key part of being able to support your child over the long term.

5. Your reality versus their reality

Partnering helps you to build a shared language and vision over time, but, in the early days, your reality and your child's may be very different. The way that you see the world and the things that are important to you may not have the same relevance to them.

The reality to them of their illness may not be what we see, because it's so personal and unique to each individual. Can you pause on being 'right' about what your child should be doing and explore some of the reasons why they are doing what they are? Consider any pressures, expectations, external forces like friends or precedent in your family to do certain things, and see if that helps you stand in their shoes. Even if you struggle to see their reality, the simple act of acknowledging there is an alternative to yours can be valid and important enough.

Move into Acceptance

Coming to terms with any new truth can be challenging and, when Issy became ill, I found it difficult and painful to let go of the present I had known and the future I had planned. While friends talked about their children's plans, I was left nursing a gaping wound where my hopes for Issy had once been. I tended that loss for a long time and it kept me stuck in a place where I couldn't move towards any kind of acceptance. Accepting that the future wasn't going to happen in the way I'd expected or, on the darkest days, conceiving of any kind of future beyond the next moment took enormous resolve.

Knowing the facts and being able to accept them can be two entirely different things. Not being able to accept what we were facing was a really natural reaction – if I didn't accept it, maybe it wasn't really happening. And maybe I could save us all some pain. But a lack of acceptance kept me in a disempowered state for months, where I hankered for a past that didn't exist and longed for a future we had little chance of living. By not accepting Issy's reality, I was inadvertently invalidating her feelings, even though, in my mind, I was shielding her from a harsh truth. By not accepting, I was making things harder for us both, and I couldn't begin to step down and partner her through.

What is acceptance?

Acceptance is recognising a situation without having to change it or fix it. It isn't necessarily liking what we face, or endorsing it, or wanting it. It's not apathy or capitulation. It is a *compassionate act* that takes away some of the judgement and pressure about what's right and how we should act, so that we can do what's needed. And we can choose to do it to ease our pain while we process the difficult emotions about what is going on.

By choosing to accept what is really going on, we are gifting ourselves and our child the opportunity to deal with what is in front of us, without judgement. Coming to acceptance is a process and, over time, it can slow the incessant questions of why and how and WTF. Accepting where we are today quietens our minds and gives us space to do what is needed to help our child and ourselves, and make some of the behavioural changes we'll look at in the next chapter.

Finding it hard to accept?

Maybe you're finding it hard to accept too? Maybe there's just too much emotion or pain around the facts of your child's mental health? Maybe you feel indignant that life as you knew it has changed? Maybe you don't feel you have the strength to follow the different path that may be necessary for your child's health and well-being? Acceptance of these situations, along with changes to our family life, our plans and how we see ourselves, takes time to process and can feel as if we're in some way giving up or giving in. If you need support, please reach out to a trusted friend, a support network like Parenting Mental Health, or a counsellor or therapist.

Accepting your child

Accepting that your child isn't either their illness or their behaviour takes some of the pressure off you both. You may find them acting in ways that feel defiant and an affront to the rules of your house or the way you live your life (gaming into the night, baking at 3am, fighting you about schoolwork, closing themselves off from the family, etc.). These actions aren't generally done to spite or annoy us. They tend to be reactions to their feelings and ways to find some peace and calm. Accepting them in a non-judgemental way can reduce the friction between you.

Accepting the situation

Accepting the situation isn't going to perpetuate it or make it worse. This isn't an admission of guilt or a statement that you approve of, enjoy or asked for what is going on. While you might not want what is happening, accepting that your child is struggling with their mental health and some of the activities they once breezed through can release you, and it can release them. True acceptance, without the need to fix, gives us space to begin to consider how we can support our family better.

Accepting YOU

Acceptance of the role we play is incredibly important if we're going to be able to change our approach to our child and the situation, and stop berating ourselves for things that we've done that we now can't change. Accepting yourself as you are – without guilt or judgement – takes practice and kindness. It might go against the way you feel about yourself and the responsibility you feel you should take, or it may not be something you're used to doing. In time, you may see that acceptance gives you space to consider what you have gained from this unwelcome episode – more connection with the right people, a deep sense of personal satisfaction or, like me, caring less about what others think of you. Everyone will win if you can bring acceptance to all of yourself.

Let's Talk About Trust

From about the time they start high school, the trust between you and your child is an evolving thing. From juggling schoolwork with a social life, to experimenting and new experiences, your child is on a path to explore the world *their* way. Your child might not want to tell you everything and they have a right to privacy.

Poor mental health can bring issues around trust to the fore, and it is something that parents mention to me time and again. Mental ill health can magnify the gaps your child *perceives* in your trust and can isolate them further. Building trust is essential if we're going to be able to travel together with our child on this journey. Trust provides our child with the belief that they can lean on us, they can share with us and they can grow a connection with us that won't change or create misunderstanding.

I value the trust I have built with Issy hugely and do all I can to respect and nurture it. And as trust is built slowly and broken quickly, it needs a careful and ongoing focus. I think of building trust in the following way:

$$\frac{\text{Consistency} + \text{Honesty} + \text{Compassion}}{\text{Time}} = \text{Trust}$$

If we are consistent, honest and compassionate, over time we can build trust:

- **Consistency** is essential if we're going to make our child feel they can share with us, no matter what they have done, not done or felt. If we can act in such a way that there is no doubt in our child's mind that they are loved and accepted, whatever they have done, we open up a powerful channel. When our child comes to know what to expect from us, they can share without fear that they've emptied the fridge, not done their chores or more serious matters too. Don't make promises only to break them later. Be consistent in your word and deed. If you say you'll do something, don't move the goalposts to try to encourage them to do more. Allow them to believe that you'll stand by what you say and that they can rely on you to do what you've said.

- **Honesty** is needed for strong trust to build, because it underpins open communication. Honesty allows you to show your vulnerability when things don't go to plan. Honesty reminds you and your child that the trust you have between you is important. It gives an opportunity to openly address the times when changes to plans or agreements are required and opens up communication. Being honest and sharing how you're feeling, or how you've failed, isn't weak. It shows humility and self-awareness, and renews your commitment to building trust with your child. Honesty is really important. Sometimes things change and we can't pick them up from school or buy the things they want. If we aren't honest, our child is likely to fill in the gaps with a mix of 'I'm not worthy' and 'Mum/Dad doesn't really care.'

- **Compassion** makes the process of building trust much easier for us and our child, because trust, like the path of mental illness, is not a straight line. As we learn to be consistent and honest, we mess up. We say yes to things we can't manage, and then we make excuses to try to make things better. We might divulge a secret not knowing it wasn't meant to be shared, or we might impatiently speak on behalf of our child in a medical or school meeting – simple things that have the power to cut the closeness we are forging and disconnect us. Being compassionate and patient with ourselves as we trip up, and spreading that compassion to our children, helps us both to understand that we aren't perfect and we're trying our hardest.

Challenge Assumptions

Assumptions are so easy to fall into. When our daughter became ill, my husband Ross desperately wanted to make everything right. A conversation with a psychiatrist changed his approach. In the course of discussing her diagnosis, Ross said to the psychiatrist that Issy would, of course, have to cope with mental illness for the rest of her life.

The psychiatrist was horrified. She explained that our daughter was her own person, with her own future as yet unwritten. She told him that there was no reason to think that she would follow in his footsteps, good or bad, in any facet of her life.

This simple statement challenged his perceptions and he recognised that he had made an assumption: Ross had assumed she would inherit his history. But our children are individual. Yes, there are genetic predispositions, but there isn't a future mapped out and locked down. If we believe something, it reinforces our approaches and behaviour.

So, ask yourself, what assumptions are you making about your child? Are you assuming they will be ill forever? Are you assuming the behaviours they display that you don't like are to annoy you or that they're risk-taking, irresponsible tearaways? Are you assuming they have control over their illness?

Assumptions can happen because we can be so desperate to see the glimmers of hope (see page 111) that we roll out today's reality and expect it to evolve. Whether it's about your child managing to get into school for an hour or a day, having a shower, seeing people, or something else that they can find so challenging when they are ill, assumptions have the power to isolate at a time when they and we are both crying out for connection and understanding.

For example, Issy would do something that she hadn't been able to face the previous day, week or month, and in my rush to see progress and not lose that sense of momentum, I assumed this was now a behaviour she could continue. I'd change my behaviour to accommodate the new capability that I expected to see again, and not only did that disappoint me, it angered and frustrated her. It disconnected us from each other at a time when we really needed to be side by side.

We can find ourselves assuming, in our desperation for progress, that this new behaviour is now possible every day, whereas it can often be a trial run, not a commitment to change.

The mental sketch pad

So why do we rush to make assumptions? Why do we want to rush ahead? Our brains are pattern-matching constantly. They are looking at what we face and are attempting to make sense of it by matching it to something from our mental archives. Our prefrontal cortex, at the front of the brain, is where we make these decisions and pattern matches. According to Amy Arnsten, PhD Professor of Neuroscience and Psychology at Yale University School of Medicine, 'The prefrontal cortex intelligently regulates our thoughts, actions and emotions through extensive connections with other brain regions. It creates a "mental sketch pad" that can maintain information in the absence of environmental stimulation. Neuroscientists refer to this process as working memory: the ability to keep in mind an event that has just occurred, or bring to mind information from long-term storage, and use this representational knowledge to regulate behaviour, thought and emotion.'

When it comes to assumptions about our child's behaviour, we're drawing from our mental sketch pad. When they were a baby and started crawling, we saw progress and knew they would walk at some point. When they learned to ride a bike, their confidence and proficiency grew over time. They moved forward. And thanks to our own knowledge and experiences, we could realistically predict that our assumptions about their progress were accurate and they would continue on.

Enter mental illness, and all of those experiences you're drawing from are now incongruent, irrelevant and in a foreign language. They don't compute. Not only are the memories on your mental sketch pad outdated, they simply don't make any sense.

If your child couldn't leave the house yesterday or the week or even the month before, and yet today they managed a few minutes in the garden or declared they were meeting a friend, in between whoops of relief and delight our mental sketch pad searches for experiences to help us respond to this. It finds one: linear progress. But this is wrong, because, as we've seen, mental illness is not linear. Voicing these assumptions diminishes the achievement and turns it into an obligation.

This situation and your expectation of a repeat performance can leave your child feeling so alone. They can feel that you don't understand what they're facing and, worse still, it can come across to them as if they are being judged. Perhaps they've been building up to doing something and, rather than being met with acceptance, they are met with obligation. The obligation of your assumptions and disappointment.

Suddenly, rather than being able to celebrate that achievement, they feel the pressure to continue it, to keep it up and improve. They feel a disconnection between you and them and their recovery, because your actions can leave them feeling you lack empathy for the daily challenges they face.

Try seeing your child as you would a friend's child; full of potential and possibility. Lean on memories of them as their younger selves, when the only overwhelm came from pure physical exhaustion, rather than the constant Inquisition playing out in your mind now.

Living 'adaptively'

One way to combat assumptions is to live 'adaptively'. If your child can do something on a certain day, you *adapt* to the limits of what they can do on that particular day. When you wake up tomorrow, you have a whole new day ahead of you, another blank slate, and you see how things are today. It is a much easier and happier place to be than the rollercoaster of assumptions.

If your child agrees to do something that is usually difficult for them – maybe going shopping or having dinner together at home – see the desire to do it as a win. If they join in and suddenly the mood changes, it's OK. Don't try to guilt them into change – this only reinforces disconnection. Think how you'd feel if someone overlooked how you felt and pushed and pushed. If they are struggling to go through with something, be their ear if they want to talk or nurture them if they don't. When things are calm, gently say there's always another chance to try, and it's OK.

Am I enabling negative behaviour?

I'm often asked if 'accepting' where a child is now is somehow 'enabling' them and their behaviour. Enabling keeps your child from learning from the negative fallout of their behaviours, but it presupposes that they are in a place to act. You know your child and whether they can't do something or don't want to do something. I never saw being compassionate to Issy's needs as enablement. She wanted to do the things she couldn't, but simply couldn't at that time. As the darkness lifted, it became easier for her to try, but also for her to explain how she was feeling and what conditions she needed for her to be in a place to try. Know that this stage is not forever. Allow your child to engage how their mental illness allows them to. It will change; it did for us.

Glimmers of Hope

There were times when Issy was ill when I got a kind of tingling in my fingers. It was as if my body was sending me a sense of anticipation, usually when something had changed or was changing. It might have been a simple yes to something I offered, like changing her bedding, or sharing something that had helped her. I call these positive situations 'glimmers'. I think that glimmers shoot in (and often straight out!) to remind you that progress is possible and to help you hold on to the potential for change.

Like assumptions, glimmers are generally not to be shared with your child. Fragile and evanescent to us, they can morph from joy to obligation in as long as it takes for you to ask your child how or why they did what led to the glimmer's creation or when it will happen again. Speaking about these moments can set off a range of reactions in your child, mainly about being watched and viewed as some kind of lab rat. Glimmers are important to us parents, but our children generally need to see their progress on their terms.

Glimmers don't always shine bright. Sometimes glimmers simply hold the smallest hint of a glow. They can be the potential of an appointment to discuss next steps or a simple 'yes' to a cup of tea, a drive or a hug. Hold on to these glimmers, but see them for what they are: fireflies along the path to recovery. They aren't a beacon or a signal of recovery. Let them be what they are – beautiful sparks that remind you that things change and there is hope.

Why we need to celebrate the changes

Partnering your child through mental illness is about acknowledging what's really going on and accepting the alternatives you are putting in place, the things you're finding strange or different, and how those are changing. Celebrating the changes to those situations is a powerful reminder that nothing lasts and that change is all around us.

The more you celebrate those differences, the more important and resonant they will become to you, not just now, but in the future. The acceptance you show your child and the recognition you give to the things they feel, think and do that matter to them can become meaningful memories for you both.

I never expected to celebrate my daughter getting a train alone aged 16 for the first time in years. But the day she did it, I sobbed with the greatest joy. I was unashamedly proud, still a bit scared that something would send her back into depression, but beyond delighted for the progress this signified.

We're one weak smile away from knowing what is truly important in the world. When your child's face says thank you for backing me up, for believing in me, for being there when no one else is, you realise that connection and commitment with those you love is just everything.

Managing Your Expectations

If a child feels that they constantly have to perform, how can we expect them to begin to heal? Taking the pressure off your child, giving them the space to begin to come to terms with their feelings, is something you can do for them at a time when many parents often feel impotent. Whether the emotions they use to communicate with you are through tiredness, frustration, anger, or all of the associated symptoms of depression and anxiety, a release of pressure or expectation gives them an opportunity to just *be*. It gives them time to consider recovery and their first steps towards progress.

How can we expect them to begin to understand themselves if they are constantly fighting us, themselves, their illness, the norms and the expectations?

Our job as parents is to create a safe space where our children are supported, where they are believed in, where they are nurtured and where they are loved. That safe space is not always on our terms; sometimes it's on their terms, sometimes it's on other people's, but it is born from a love of them and a desire to act in their best interests. Those best interests might not be what everybody else wants or expects. They might not be what the school says is the right thing, or what your grandmother thinks they should be doing, or even what you think is right.

If we can pause and reflect on the ways we interact and step down from the authority position, we can become better at understanding their needs; we can stand beside them as they make their own sense of this time, on their terms. We can build rock-solid trust that opens up a safe space where we can appreciate each other's point of view and our child feels safe to look their mental health issues in the eye. Changing the way we interact with our child isn't just about getting them through mental illness; it's about building a shared bond that validates them as the whole, worthy, wonderful human they are, and connects us beyond this time.

Boundaries

'A boundary is a circle around that which is sacred, and you get to decide what that is.'

Elizabeth Gilbert

Many of the parents I work with wish that there was a definitive line around boundaries, but sadly there isn't. Boundaries are a battleground of parenting. Give in to the boundaries you set and you're seen as a light touch, but be militant about them and they lead to disconnection and dissent. It's hard to get this one right!

When your child is mentally ill, the lack of control they feel can manifest as intolerance to your boundaries. They ignore your boundaries on behaviour or they don't see the boundaries you place around your own self-care or privacy. They can see your sacred circle as a high wall and try to scale it in search of connection.

We can set unrealistic boundaries around what we expect of our children when they are ill. Partnering them requires us to understand what's possible and adjust our boundaries accordingly. When we see that their inability to agree and comply is a product of their illness, rather than a direct insult, it helps us to take a more compassionate approach to their behaviour.

When Issy had disclosed her suicide intent, I had to change my 'boundary' about going to the bathroom alone! She was scared and needed constant reassurance that the feelings she had weren't going to consume her. I was happy to lower my boundaries around privacy to accommodate her needs. Equally, when she was in crisis, I accepted more flexible boundaries around things like sleep where she slept longer and later than before. You'll have your own boundaries that serve your needs, and it's for you to find your balance and what works for you and your child.

When our child defines a boundary, this is an opportunity for them to exercise control. If we can acknowledge it, whether it is the need to cook their own food, not allow you access to their room or decide they are incapable of doing something or being somewhere, we can validate their needs and positively reinforce that they do have some control. This may seem a small thing to do, but it has far-reaching impacts and can be a step towards them believing they have agency to change and recovery.

Protecting yourself

When boundaries are breached with violence or aggression, this is never acceptable. Your safety and peace should always remain sacred, so ensure you are not in danger. If needs be, call the police, a friend or school, and prioritise yourself if this is happening.

When boundaries are challenged, we can often see the parts of ourselves that aren't healed as people. Maybe we weren't shown how to maintain effective boundaries with love and so we give in, because we don't have the language to explore what is going on. Maybe we become indignant, affronted and angry that our rights aren't being respected, because we weren't empowered as children to have a voice and expect to have it as a parent. When your boundaries are challenged, which they will be during this journey, ask yourself *why* this is challenging you and what your child is trying to communicate. If 'all behaviour is communication', what is your child trying to say to you? What do they need from you that your boundary isn't allowing? And what does your reaction want you to know?

When it's OK to protect your boundaries

It's a balance to know when to allow your child to break your boundaries, when to let them into your 'circle'. The thing that is sacred to you may not be for them. Ensuring that our psychological, physical, mental and spiritual needs are met, through regular, committed self-care, therapy or connection with the people who make us feel safe and loved, can help us gain perspective on which boundaries are worth the fight for our own self and which can be opened up for our child's best interests.

If boundaries are something you struggle with, challenge yourself to find something that is meaningful to you and draw a circle around it, protect it. Enlist help to ensure it remains so, whether it's your weekly shift at work or your regular trip to the hairdresser. And know that for every boundary you set and maintain, not to the detriment of your child, you are showing them that you are valuable and, by association, so are they.

Keep in mind . . .

1. Changing your behaviour can really help your child during this time. 'Partnering' is a new way of thinking about parenting and it can be a positive way to move forward.

2. By acknowledging where you are today, you can let go of expectations and assumptions that might be holding you and your child back.

3. Adapting and managing your own expectations at this time can be a powerful thing. It can give you and your child the chance to build trust and work your way through this, together.

4. Boundaries may change during this time. You may need to review your existing boundaries, and protect others.

5. Notice and celebrate the positive changes you see.

8

Building Connection Through Communication

Speak to your child in the ways you want to be spoken to. Respect their space. Communicate with love.

Have you ever found that others don't grasp what you really mean and that your intent is misconstrued? This is even more easily done when you're communicating with someone with a mental illness and when you're under huge pressure to manage your own stress. Communication is absolutely essential to trust and close connections, so in this chapter, we'll look at this in more depth.

A time of disconnection

Really connecting with teenagers isn't always easy at the best of times. At an age when our children *should* be moving off and exploring independence, we can find that mental illness makes communication even harder. It may present us with someone who needs constant support and reinforcement. Or they may want more space. It is easy to feel disconnected with them and not know how we can support them. We can wonder *how* to communicate with them, so we can connect and not feel more distant from them.

Communication was key throughout Issy's illness, and it wasn't always a two-way conversation. There were many times when it felt like I was the only one communicating and I wondered if she was even hearing me. But she was, and the tone and nature of my words and actions was vital to building a connection to support her through to recovery.

We experienced the entire spectrum of connection when Issy became ill, from the earliest days when she needed to be with us all the time, to the darkest times when she couldn't find the words to tell me that she intended to end her life.

As much as we may want our child to share with us, having a child with mental illness can bring its own challenges. The everyday privacy and autonomy we come to expect – like waking up on our terms – can diminish, or even disappear. It can feel like we have a fully grown newborn to care for, with the same levels of dependence and urgency as a baby. And this can lead to frustration, which can boil over into annoyance, one of the least useful emotions for anyone who wants to open up communication channels.

Communicating successfully with a child with a mental illness needs you to be selfless. You need to overlook what you may perceive as selfish or irresponsible behaviour. You need to see that it's about them and not you. When a child is behaving in a way that you find difficult to understand, try to remember that they're not seeking attention, they're seeking a *connection*. How can your words help them? How might your words harm that? And all behaviour is communication. What are they telling you?

A New Way to Communicate

Making sense of what our child means and needs is really challenging, because we can't rely on our assumptions (see page 283) or, if we're partnering (see Chapter 6), fall back on our position as the authority who has the last word. It breaks down trust and connection. Be curious, not closed when you're speaking with your child and keep in mind the view of the healthy and positive vision you want to move towards.

In any moment, we have the power to change how we respond and react. The way we communicate with our children may have changed, but so can we. Let's look at how we can make communication flow more easily and allow deeper understanding.

Choose your words carefully

When you're first faced with a hint of a mental health issue, you may feel communication is non-existent. You're not being told about the feelings or events that have contributed to this, so seeing the outputs of anxiety, depression or an eating or other disorder laid bare can feel hugely frustrating. It might seem like it's all about 'difficult' conversations that need to happen – something else that is a barrier to connection.

There is good news. Mental illness can be the catalyst for *better* communication. Yes, that's right. Through this process you can learn how to move towards a deep and meaningful understanding between you and your child. It takes practice and is often counter-intuitive, but it is possible.

Language is a blunt tool that we use in our busy lives to make life run smoothly. By the time the teenage years kick in, we as parents can find we're communicating in the main about things that ensure we deliver on our commitments to life – school, work, family. We can find ourselves speaking in clichés and generalities, and it's easily done; they have become a common and accepted language that glosses over nuanced meaning and understanding. Notice how when someone meets your teenager when out and about, they usually ask them, 'How's school?' It is easy for us all to get into those same habits.

Basic questions like this don't give us a deep understanding. They can leave an air of insincerity, they don't build connection and they leave a gap between what we hear and what we know and feel to be true. If we can't use language that is a true reflection of what we're feeling, how can we expect our children to answer with anything other than a shrug or 'sure'?

Being as accurate as possible in your communications with your child (and everyone involved) can help build trust, remove the likelihood of misunderstandings and take away some of the roles we assume so we can open up meaningful and worthwhile conversations.

For example, how many times have you replied 'fine' when asked how you are? How does that engender openness or start a meaningful conversation with someone? And more, what does it say to you about yourself? How do you feel when you drum all of your feelings down and encapsulate them in a simple 'fine'?

We tend to use generic language because we're desperate; desperate to communicate quickly and get our point across, to connect, to fix, to effect a change. Our language can also be a sign of our impatience or impotence. Have you ever said: 'I'm just trying to help'? This phrase is more about you than about your child. Even though the ultimate outcome is their health and well-being, the intent can appear to be all about you and it can isolate your child further.

Ask quality questions

Open questions, that allow for more than a 'yes' or 'no' reply, are helpful to open up conversation. They can take time to consider and practice to master. If we're not careful they can become accusative or judgemental. Any question with 'why' at the start of it can feel like an obligation to a teenager, and it's so easy to shut down connection if they think they're just being interrogated by us.

Questions can also be veiled attempts to get our child to do something – consider if you're implicitly *telling* your child something, while pretending to ask a question of them.

Being open to hearing the answer can also be a challenge. Listening to what our child wants to say to us, without judgement, takes practice. Ask yourself if you're ready to hear all they have to say.

Your child can easily sniff out questions with a deeper intent. However innocent your intention, questions such as the following tend to be seen as directions, not questions:

- When are you going to start going to bed earlier?
- When are you going to start waking up earlier?
- Do you think it would be a good idea if . . .
- Would you like me to get your school uniform ready?
- Would you like me to bring the hoover up?
- Can you let me know when you want to have a shower?
- Why do you spend so much time on your phone/ computer?
- Have you used that new shampoo I bought last week?

Take the emotion out of what you say

Our words to our poorly children can seem like the most expedient way of communicating how much we care and how we feel about them, but our words can be loaded and become a weapon, directed at the wrong person.

Try to take the emotion out of interactions. It's easier said than done, but accepting that you're in this space and that your words can hurt or heal helps you to see the power in them. Maybe you've spent all day worrying and the emotional build-up explodes when your child leaves a dirty cup in the freshly tidied living room. It could be that you've been waiting to go out with them and they decide at the last minute that they can't, or you can't let their spending all their time in their room, which you perceive as isolation, pass without comment: 'Do you think I exist to clean up after you?', 'I've been waiting all day to see you!' or 'Do you really think online friends are real friends?' all leave your child in no doubt that you don't get it, or them, or their challenges, and serve only to bring the shutters down and distance you further.

If you can't contain yourself, consider the ways you can release the feelings before they bubble over and you blurt out the 'wrong' thing. Many times, it's when we don't acknowledge that these feelings exist that they explode when we're triggered by an action or a comment from our child.

Try not to project your fears and feelings into a conversation. The fact that your child doesn't want to eat what you've cooked doesn't mean they will never eat again or that they hate your cooking. If your words carry the weight of your fears and concerns, they will be given to your child and won't help either of you.

Finding New Ways to Talk

Sometimes the best conversations happen when we're not face to face. It might be when sorting out a cupboard or prepping dinner. You could send a text or a link to something you've found. We had emojis that Issy used. One meant 'I don't want to talk' and one meant 'I need to'. These avenues can give you an insight into what's going on with your child and can grow into a safe space for you to have conversations that are otherwise hard.

Change the language

Let's take an example. If your child has said that they don't want to go to school today, and you respond:

1. 'That's OK for you!'
   The subtext here is: 'but I still have to go to work and keep going even when I don't feel like it. Why can't you?'
2. 'That's OK for you' [said with a grumble]
   The subtext here is: 'I have to deal with the school! You have no idea how hard it is having to cope with your behaviour and their judgement.'
3. 'That's OK, I suppose.'
   The subtext here is: 'I'm unsure, but I don't know what to say instead of that.' This leaves your child feeling unsure if you're on their side, if they are doing the right thing and isolates you both further.
4. 'It's OK' [said calmly, lovingly, with a smile]
   The subtext here is: 'I understand that something is happening to you. I don't know how it feels, but I care about you.' Your child will feel heard, supported and shielded from any repercussions.

Consider how you can change your language or tone (because sometimes it's all about the delivery) to ensure you say what your child needs to hear.

It's normal to feel . . .

It's normal to feel frustration when you can't fix something. It's normal to feel overwhelming stress when you're concerned you will lose your child or can't see a way through this time. But it's not helpful to only let those feelings surface when you're faced with a situation that doesn't feel right or when you're dealing with your child. Holding on to being 'normal' and having to swallow the feelings and emotions that come with the tussle of being in an abnormal state is a stretch too far when you're caring for a child with a mental illness. Let yourself off the hook. Let your emotions out, with wild abandon, but in a private space. Don't delegate your own worries and fears to your child.

Deciding when to speak and when not to speak

One thing I learned early on was that not everything needs to be said, and not everything needs to be said *now*. For example, at one point, Issy's medical team started to discuss an inpatient stay. We decided not to discuss this with her yet. Had I told my daughter at the time, I think it would have broken her even more than she already was. It didn't need to be said. She didn't need the weight of that decision, particularly when she could have perceived it as the choice being taken from her by CAMHS.

Recently, when Issy and I were discussing a report about the numbers of young people being admitted, I explained that we had taken the decision to challenge CAMHS on a stay in a unit and decided to nurse her at home. She was grateful for the decision but also that we hadn't burdened her with the choice at the time. She said she felt that she was overwhelmed with information at a time when she was trying to make sense of her illness, and this would have been an obligation.

In another example, we decided to sit Issy for some GCSEs to help her meet the entry levels for college admission. At the time, she was so much better than she had been, yet looking back I see how far she still had to go. Her brain capacity had been impacted on by her depression and challenges with eating and she couldn't take in huge amounts of information. It exasperated her.

I chose not to overwhelm her with more information. She didn't need to know the finer details of the exam day, where we'd park or what we'd do beforehand. She didn't need me to say that I'd read that the exams were harder this year. She didn't need to hear anything that would rock her stability.

Maybe your child needs a haircut, a shower, a decent meal, a room fumigation? Maybe they *really* do! But ask yourself: what good will telling them that do? They're not stupid. They know they smell, or need feeding, or live in the domestic equivalent of a cesspit, but they have more pressing things to consider at the moment.

Is telling them that going to help? What outcome are you trying to achieve by saying it? Are you trying to make them feel better, or you?

Trying to understand the bigger fight they're facing is essential if you're going to connect. Look beyond your own disappointment or disgust and ask: What can I do to support them now? What do they need? I can guarantee it isn't you nagging them to clean their room. Your job is to support them through their difficulties, not to be 'right'.

Maybe you're thinking 'my house, my rules'. If our children don't have a share in the house rules, we're not partnering them. If we want them to feel a sense of their own worth and security, they need to be listened to, heard and respected.

Speak to your child in the ways you want to be spoken to. Respect their space. Communicate with love. Look at your child and ask: How can I help you? What can I do to support you better? Then reflect on the changes in your child.

Monitoring without managing

One of the things that we struggled with in the early days of Issy's illness was over-managing. We'd take the temperature every time we engaged with her and, before long, it became a point of annoyance for her. 'Are you OK?' said with the urgency of an overwhelmed, concerned parent is a sure-fire way to kick-start an eyeball marathon and raise the barriers between you.

Listening for cues is essential in partnering and, because of the duration of most mental health issues, it's important to keep perspective on these signals. When something happens that is different, mark it down. Don't stress over it if you miss recording something; this is about giving you something to reflect upon, not beat yourself up about. Keeping a note of cues can help keep your sense of perspective, serve as a record for when meeting with professionals and also stop you from having to ask *the* question. You might see patterns start to emerge, perhaps with hormone cycles (in both boys and girls), and this might help you identify which events, people, food and even expectations trigger certain responses in your child.

Being present

I know there were many times in my children's early lives that my own 'busyness' stopped me from being fully present. As I get older, I understand why when they were young, stacking those bricks together, mindfully, for what felt like the thousandth time, was so important. And why being present in every sense in the middle of the night was a gift, even when it felt like anything but that.

The time when someone says to you, please be here for me, and you are present, connects you in a way that cannot be changed. It forges bonds as strong as titanium. The times you are present connect you to your child in a special way. These times offer you the privilege of sharing a personal moment or a confidence and building a new shared memory. Being present is one of the loudest ways you can share that you care, that someone matters and you will get through together.

Getting comfortable with 'no'

As the parent of a child with a mental illness, hearing the word 'no' will become a recurring experience. Whether it's your child saying no to going out, to having a shower, to talking, eating, sleeping, trying ... 'no' is safety in their eyes. No doesn't challenge. It doesn't change anything, so it feels safe to them. Getting comfortable with this is hard, but necessary. If you can shift to suggesting things, rather than demanding, it will help make the negative responses less painful and less of a judgement on your abilities, and therefore easier for you to bear.

As a parent, you might have to get used to saying 'no' too. You might have to say no to events that take you away from home, no to family who want to visit, to holidays, to work, to friends and fun. It's tough. If you think that each 'no' for you is a reflection of your commitment to your child, it can make it feel a little easier and a little less permanent.

The Power of Patience

Patience is the fuel of partnering. Patience can be so hard to find when you're angry at the challenges you're faced with. You want to rush through the stages and fix everything now. You can have *some* influence over the duration of your child's illness, but you can't rush it. If you ignore mental health, deny it, minimise it or expect your child to carry on living and learning as they may have done in the past, you are going to slow this right down, and potentially send it into hiding so it never gets addressed. Every time we try to force our child into something that does not support their mental health, we can be delaying recovery. Impatience can steepen the curve and accelerate the descent. The more desperate we become to try to hold on to 'normality', the less control we have to effect change.

Human optimism can be helpful to make us believe in recovery, but it can also prevent us from accepting the whole situation and embracing new behaviours.

Patience is a recurring theme in this new world of partnering, and it does get easier, the more you do it. When our children can't explain what they mean, patience becomes an even more vital skill. We need to be patient with our children as they make sense of what they're facing. When we ask what they feel, need, believe, want or hope for, they generally don't know. They're having to uncover their feelings and make sense of this new and difficult emotional landscape. Have patience with them as they excavate themselves. Our bright, creative, smart, amazing children get even more frustrated because they can't articulate that the argument you're having with them isn't going to work. Be open and direct in your communication. Be kind and generous with your responses.

What Not to Say (Probably)

I asked the amazing parents in the Parenting Mental Health community what they regretted saying, what missed the mark when communicating with their children. Below are just some of their responses. Of course, some of these may work for you and your child, and others may not – it's a personal thing:

- 'For me, it doesn't work if I say "I'd like you to . . ." It always brings the shutters down. It makes her feel bad and she can't cope with that!'
- 'I believe the phrase "Don't do . . ." to be unhelpful.'
- ' "How are you feeling?" is a no-no for us.'
- 'The phrase, "It's OK, I understand . . ." is a definite no-no for us.'
- ' "I get what you're going through" always sends J into a rage, or "I'm here if you need me".'
- 'I think asking questions in general is a no. Silence is golden; don't always feel you have to fill it. Give them time to think about what they want to tell you. "I'm sorry you feel like that" or "I understand" works better. I also find giving her a choice blows her brain: "Have you any idea what might have triggered it?" '
- 'Any questions at all are a no-go here. I have to just leave him in peace if he is low and let him come to me. I have to just listen and not really say much. If I respond with anything other than a casual "nice one", "that sounds crap" or "that sucks" then the shutters come down.'
- ' "I can't help you if I don't know what's wrong" breaks my daughter every single time as she doesn't even know what's wrong herself. So, it makes her feel like no one can help her.'

- ' "Could I suggest you try . . . ?" I said that to my daughter once and she flew at me verbally with "What makes you know how I feel to even suggest anything?" I was suggesting the breathing techniques to help reduce the panic attack I could see developing. Now if I see her going into one I just stand by her doing the breathing and then she usually follows.'

- ' "I am disappointed that you . . ." could be anything from you didn't clean your room, didn't do your homework, etc. That phrase would always upset my daughter.'

Sometimes say nothing at all

It's also worth remembering that sometimes it's best to say nothing. Silence is as much of a communicator as speaking. It can say I respect your space, privacy and the challenges you face, and I have the time and desire to hear you. Silence can be a way of communicating acceptance and love or disappointment and disagreement. Consider how you can make it the former.

Listen to Understand, Not to Respond

Setting aside our innate need to control and be right, particularly when we're dealing with our children, is a challenge. And whether you feel that you're in charge or they are, ultimate understanding comes when we listen to and really, deeply, hear them.

'Most people do not listen with the intent to understand. They listen with the intent to reply.'

Stephen Covey

Allowing your child to be heard is one of the most connective and giving things you can do for them. In our rush to fix, we can be quick to diminish or explain away our child's feelings, removing the opportunity for them to be heard and for us to connect. Sometimes we only want to hear what we feel is going to help us move forward and resolve stuff. We can't imagine taking on any more trauma or stress and so we half-listen without commitment or investment.

As the battle you are fighting together is *their* mental illness, it is so important to listen to *them*. Being heard, believed and validated can serve as a battery boost for your child. Allow their thoughts and feelings to tumble from their mouths. It might sound like a new language that none of you speak or want to learn, and your child's words or needs might not make sense to you, but they need you to bear witness to them. It is important to them, it shows they are important to you and serves to cleanse them as much as possible of the feelings and the fear that are generated on a daily basis when mental illness is present.

> When your child comes to you and wants to get their thoughts out, whatever they are, however ridiculous or unlikely or unreasonable they may seem to you, please listen, please hear them.

Being heard was a big deal for me and for Issy too. Being able to talk at me whenever she needed to, day or (generally in the middle of the) night, to allow the jumbled mess of thoughts to tumble out of her, was the ultimate show and growth of trust between us. And whenever it happened, it always felt like a gift. Whether it was a rant about something she considered unjust or that she had made peace or a breakthrough with something that had led to her being ill and needed to share, she needed the validation of being heard, and that was something to treasure for me. It meant the door to connection was open and there was a chance to understand her more. And when a child comes to you and asks you to stop them from overdosing, as Issy did, you'll see the benefits of being open all-hours to them.

How to listen well

Giving your attention to someone is one of the best ways of showing your love and their value. So, how do you listen well? 'Active listening' is an approach used by many counsellors and therapists that enables strong bonds to form and trust to be built, enabling the speaker to feel comfortable with opening up.

The first stage with active listening is to create a safe space that gives your child the signal that it's OK to share and open up. Sometimes the best conversations happen in the places where there is no eye contact, like in the car, or in the kitchen chopping veggies, or when decorating or clearing out the garage. Sometimes we need the veil of movement to enable our words to flow and to cover any embarrassment.

It's really important that you're not 'listening but not listening' while trying to watch your favourite box set, for example. Being led by your child is key here; if they come in and sit on the sofa, when they are normally not seen outside of their room, and want to talk, give them your attention. Put your phone down. Turn the volume down. We can all rewind the last episode of *Game of Thrones*, but we can't play back this moment with our child.

As the listener, you need to concentrate fully on what is being said but also on what is being conveyed. Look at your child's body language. Sometimes it doesn't match the words they're saying. Think of yourself as a parental Poirot or Miss Marple and seek out what's really going on. Not to judge, or fix, or challenge, but simply to understand.

The opposite of active listening is 'passive fixing': you don't listen to understand or even respond, you hear to fix. We've all been there: You're busy. You have heard their rant about a friend or a teacher, or whatever, a million times. You've just relaxed after a long day when they come and want to share their innermost fears and thoughts. You have a finite window to build and nurture trust, so set that duster aside and focus on them. If interesting people have messy houses, so do good listeners.

A top tip to help with your active listening is 'mirroring'. Mirroring is a way of building trust by mimicking the other person's facial expression or body language. You might find you do it naturally when you're sitting opposite someone at a dinner table. It's a simple, intuitive way to connect. And as you're listening to understand, not respond, mirroring can be a really powerful way of saying, 'I'm here and I hear you,' in a non-verbal way.

Being self-aware is really important to active listening, because how do you know you're doing it if you're not able to monitor yourself? Check your body language. Are you open? If you're crossing your legs or arms, this can be seen as a defence or barrier to connection.

If the impression we give is one of boredom or disdain, it might appear to our child that we're belittling what they are saying. If so, it's the start of a breakdown in trust and them feeling alienated. If you find yourself sighing heavily, eye-rolling, fidgeting or yawning, imagine what message your child gets from that.

Consider how you respond to your child. Make eye contact, nod when appropriate and say words like 'yes', 'mmm', 'uh huh' – whatever feels comfortable and natural to you. There is no need to respond verbally unless asked to. This is about allowing your child to say what they want to say. This is about you understanding what is really going on and not jumping in with a fix or solution. This is not about judging their words or actions. It is about communicating empathy, trust and understanding.

Don't be afraid of some silence. Don't jump in, ready to fix. Sit there with that silence. That's where the thinking takes place and shared understanding is created. Check your reactions in that silence. A smile or a nod can make all the difference to how your child feels about themselves and what they are sharing.

Another technique you can try is 'replaying'. Replaying or repeating what your child has said to you is a simple way to ensure you have understood what they are trying to convey. It can be helpful for them to hear back what they have said. Sometimes it takes someone else to precis our thoughts before we can make sense of them ourselves. Use phrases like, 'So what you're saying is . . . ', 'I understand you feel . . . ', 'Am I right in thinking you feel . . . ?' to allow them to clarify what they really think and to aid your understanding. Remember this is about them feeling heard and safe and not judged. It will also help you expand your understanding so that you can support them in a positive and appropriate way.

What to avoid with active listening

Interrupting isn't generally a positive behaviour as an active listener. When we're trying to get our point across, it means we're not in the moment, we're not immersed in what they are trying to share with us. If we need to say something, it is usually because there is an appropriate pause. If your child is talking, there's not a lack of conversation, so there's really no need to interrupt.

Active listening is not judgemental. It is not a way of seeing how your child feels through the lens of your own values. It is a wonderful gift you can give them, and anyone, that says their words and feelings and reactions are valid and heard.

And what if they say something you don't approve of? What if they tell you they're taking drugs, or stealing from their sibling, aren't going to school, or any number of things that would seriously impact on your ability as the parent to be a calm, active listener?

Preparation is really helpful with this, and it goes back to acknowledgment of the situation and being a partner to them. It's unlikely that you will not have any gut feels that something is going on. Your A-grade student generally doesn't come in one day explaining they've been playing truant at the local shopping centre for the past six months without some change in behaviour that you can pinpoint.

> If we remember that every child who is 'misbehaving' – and that may be as simple as not adhering to our values as parents – is seeking **connection**, not attention, taking a calm and steady approach to it will begin to open up the possibility of trust and an opportunity to find out what's really going on.

Empowering Your Child

Empowering our children to take responsibility for their actions doesn't come from *telling* them to take responsibility. If only it was that easy! If you can start opening up the conversations you have with them about things that aren't easy, or pretty, or ideal, it builds a trust that enables you to love them, without feeling angry and frustrated or feeling the need to control them. It also gives your child permission to take responsibility for their actions, to see themselves as an individual person, one with the agency to make choices and decisions – good and bad – and not simply your child whose job is to rebel and fight you.

Depending on your relationship, your child may ask you to offer advice. Beware! This isn't the opening of the floodgates for you to tell them what to do. Sometimes it's a release of tension in them and it doesn't need any reply. 'Rhetorical' was a word we added early on to Issy's vocabulary and soon it was being replayed to me, and I quickly learned that mainly she was using me as a sounding board. She would start by saying, 'It's a rhetorical question . . .' and then scope out a range of scenarios that related to her and her future, from education, to dealing with friendships and getting healthier.

If you feel it's appropriate to actually answer your child's question, try to use phrases such as:

- 'If it were me, I'd feel . . .'
- 'In a similar situation, I might consider . . .'
- 'What do you feel the options are?'
- 'How do you feel it's best resolved?'
- 'What would you suggest to someone in this situation?'

The key is to take a patient and measured approach to answering them, which I know from my experiences can be a real challenge.

Open questions challenge your child to consider their role in the situation. Empowering them to begin to see themselves as in control and part of the solution takes time and patience. But if they understand that you will ask them their opinion, it validates the fact they have an opinion worth listening to, and over time will enable them to build a solid sense of their own beliefs and 'self-solve' their challenges, or at least begin to.

Keeping the dialogue 'open' isn't always possible, particularly when they are in crisis or if they're asking unanswerable questions about their illness or recovery. Asking them very gently and quietly what they think about a certain situation, or saying that you'd like to hear their views on what to do, forges a trust and can set off a train of thought that can empower them.

Being led by your child is essential. Some of our best conversations have been when I've challenged Issy, gently and with love, to consider how she thinks, rather than just how she feels.

When you feel like losing it

If you've ever screamed at a child, you'll know that in that split second, when they are reeling from the shock and deciding how to respond (whether to cry, scream back or to shut down), you just want to press the rewind button and be a better person, a more patient, compassionate, capable parent. You want to yell apologies and hug them so hard that the sharpness of your words doesn't cut into them.

I remember one time in particular, on Issy's first day back at school after a summer overshadowed by the prospect of facing her bullies. When she got in the car at the end of that day, the first day of her fast descent into crisis, she was beside herself with emotion. She sobbed to me that she couldn't go back, that she wasn't able to cope with the bullies for another year. I said we simply had to speak to the school or nothing would change. She was ferocious in her reply that that would not be happening and, I am not proud to share this, but I lost it. Without thinking, I shouted that we couldn't live like this. We had to speak to the school. We couldn't have another year of living on tenterhooks, walking on eggshells and other painful metaphors.

As soon as I had vented my frustration, I immediately regretted it. I wasn't annoyed with her; I was annoyed with myself. I was frustrated with the school for not taking my child's welfare seriously enough. I was cross that I'd not protected her from this.

When she really needed to have my full, empathetic, unwavering support, she felt I believed it was her fault in some way. This was a warning sign to me that I was not listening well enough, either to Issy or to my own emotions about the situation. We got through it. I share this story to tell you that we don't always get it right, but we can continue to try.

I have found the most powerful ways to connect and encourage my daughter to open up to be when I suspend my own desires and the outcomes I want. Listening to a child and making them feel heard, loved and supported means putting your needs to one side momentarily so you can listen to them and be there for them.

Building Trust Through Communication

If you've acknowledged what is happening within your family and accepted it, it is much easier to begin to build trust. Acknowledging and accepting your child's mental illness is the start of a new kind of trust, but it takes time for them and you to really feel and believe it. Over time, your actions and the way you communicate helps them to trust that they can share their innermost thoughts with you, in a way that they likely wouldn't if they were not going through a mental illness. So how do we go about being consistent, honest and compassionate over time to build trust?

Work on yourself

If you've acknowledged what's going on with your child's mental health and how you influence it, it is much easier to begin to rebuild trust. Without acceptance of the situation and who you are as a person, your expectations, assumptions and reactions, it can be pretty much impossible to build trust, because your words and actions will not be aligned (see page 149).

- Think of three words to describe yourself. Don't overthink them, just write down the first three that come to mind. How happy are you with those words? Do they reflect who you want to be? Are they defined by how you were raised? Are they serving you and your family?
- Think of three more words that you'd like to describe you. Just the simple act of recognising we're not maybe

where we want to be helps us to recognise how we might be perceived and what our part in building trust can be.

Be patient

Good things take time. Building trust comes from the repeated act of consistent action. Don't expect things to change overnight and, if things flare up, as they often do, be patient when it happens. Rome wasn't built in a day, and neither is trust.

Keep believing

It's easy to be full of hope and positivity in the early days of anything new – until the things you'd expected to change don't. And then we can find ourselves second-guessing and wondering if we're ever going to have a trusting bond with our child. As their behaviour may not show the kind of open response or feedback loop we'd like, we can begin to feel dejected and wonder what the point is. Don't throw in the trust towel. Keep believing, keep being consistent and honest and compassionate, and it will grow.

Learn to apologise

When you mess up, apologise – swiftly, genuinely and without reservation or condition. Whatever has happened isn't a judgement on you or your parenting; it's a lesson that it's OK to be wrong and to admit it. We're in this game of life to keep playing, not to win.

Find a common connection

Trying something new together, where you are both challenged with new concepts, skills and ideas, is a solid way to see each other in a different light and show vulnerability. (Issy and I baked our way through our favourite cookery books.) This, in turn, fuels trust over time. Coming through a different challenge together, aside from battling mental illness, shows your child a positive side of you that they may never have seen.

Embrace your new shared language

Language enables us to understand each other, and a shared language helps us understand each other better. As trust grows, you may see a new, shared language develop – words that mean something just to you. From the words your child uses to let you understand when they intend to self-harm to a way of quickly determining mood ('rainy', 'cloudy' and 'sunny' worked for us), these words can create a connection that allows everyone to be more vulnerable and share without fear, and be a shortcut to understanding when you don't have all the answers.

Keep in mind . . .

1. Kind, consistent communication and behaviour are key to creating that connection and fighting the isolation and despair that mental illness creates. Partnering your child consistently through this time will strengthen your rapport and relationship.

2. Language – the words that you use, and the way that you say them, have an enormous impact. We can all find ways to improve and enhance our communication skills.

9

The Importance of Self-Care

You can't pour from an empty cup.

Having a positive mental attitude is more crucial than ever when your child is suffering with a mental health issue. You have the unenviable job of flying the flag of hope at this time, and if you don't believe life will improve, it's hard for your child to. But hope is hard when we're exhausted yet can't sleep, and fearful of what is next and whether we have anything left to cope with it.

Self-care sounds so 'lite' compared to the hardcore support we need, but it is so important. In many ways, I'm writing this book to show you how important *you* are in your child's journey to wellness. You are likely to be the beating heart of your family and, without you, it would not function in the same way. So, self-care is not selfish, indulgent or 'what other people do'. It must become what *you* do, for yourself, for your child and for your sanity, if you are going to make it through this and bring your family along with you.

If I send myself back to 2015 when my daughter first became suicidal and the world we knew changed, there's no way I'd have read this chapter. I would have flicked through it and then moved to find the practical bits that I would have hoped would help me 'fix' her illness.

In a time of crisis, the last thing I thought I needed or wanted was to look after myself. I just didn't have time! I thought it would take vital energy away from trying to get through every day, distract me from the job in hand: keeping her alive.

I urge you to read this chapter! I learned over the coming months that not only was self-care not selfish, it was an *essential* part of partnering Issy to recovery. In short, it gave me the necessary energy and focus I needed and, through my actions, it helped to shape the way she took care of herself and realised her value as she recovered.

We don't get given a guidebook (sadly!)

At the height of Issy's illness, there were days when I believed myself more capable of climbing Everest than getting through the night. I simply didn't have a handle on how to cope or what to expect, and the future felt uncertain, scary and way beyond my pay grade as a 'trainee' partner. Part of my fear came from the realisation that no one could tell me what to do. Why was I having to fight this unknown, alone? Why wasn't there a guidebook to mental illness in your child? Why didn't schools recognise mental illness and deal with it like they would measles or tonsillitis? Why couldn't someone help me out of the mental and emotional treacle that I was wading through, trying to find the answers to why she was ill, how we could get her through and whether she would ever recover?

Overwhelmed and underprepared, at a time when I should have been seeking solace in goodness, I was seeking comfort in food, wine and worry. Dealing with Issy's illness was binary to me; full on supporting her, completely off supporting me. I didn't see I was valuable enough to be worried about.

On more days than is healthy, as 6pm came around, if Issy was relatively calm and settled and I knew I wouldn't be driving later, I'd crack open the wine. Wine gave me permission to set down all my worries and fears and pretend Issy's illness and the resultant emotional chaos I felt wasn't happening. It was neither good for me nor sustainable and, over time, I coined a phrase to reflect its impact: 'pickled by Pinot'.

It's not my proudest moment sharing this with you, but I do so to encourage you to challenge yourself on how you're getting through. There's no shame in what you do to help yourself cope – whether it's over-shopping, a sneaky cigarette or, like me, the call of the grape at the end of the day – but the more conscious we are of these behaviours, without any judgement of whether they are right or wrong, the easier it is to bring ourselves to a more balanced and nurturing way of coping.

Why looking after yourself is so important

As Issy came out of crisis, I began to know better, and it's that experience that I'd like to share, to help you to make it through, stronger and more resilient. You need to take care of yourself for three key reasons:

1. So you can be a more present, calm and supportive parent to your child. When our needs aren't met, we can't meet our child's needs. We need to be able to cope with the uncertainty and randomness that their declining mental health deposits in our life.
2. You are the blueprint for your child, so how you show that you value yourself, in how you care for yourself, how you speak to yourself and how you notice and nurture your needs, is essential to their well-being.
3. You matter. You deserve to be cared for, and you'll feel better for it.

I'm not suggesting here that you need some kind of fixing. You don't. You are perfectly imperfect as you are, and being a human is a continuum. There's no finish line for being the best us. But you deserve to feel good about yourself, recharge and to strengthen your sense of self too. Whether that's through a connection with friends, immersion in books and films, better sleep, more sex, cultivating a greater sense of your own style, or just being gentle and kind to that face that looks back at you from the mirror, you deserve it. And it will help your child and you to get through. It won't change their illness, but it will give you more ammunition to fight it.

What is self-care?

Self-care is any activity we do to take care of our mental, emotional, spiritual and physical health. It is the way we nurture ourselves on a daily basis and refill our tanks so we're ready to face the next day and whatever that may bring. Self-care helps us to a place where we are able to help and serve others, and ourselves. Self-care should enrich, rather than diminish, our feelings of calm, happiness and self-worth. It is about making mindful and meaningful (to you) changes in the way you think about your value and your needs. It is a commitment to move towards being your best self and, like so much of partnering, it is a practice, rather than short-term fire-fighting.

Self-care benefits your child too

We want our children to be happier and do better than us, and one of the best ways to achieve this is to be their blueprint. Do you remember dressing up when you were a kid? What did you want to be? It's likely you were emulating an adult. You looked to them for clues on how to live your life, how to understand yourself and other people, how to take care of yourself, how to be human. Learning by example doesn't always lead us to pick up good habits, but some of the core traits we do learn from those around us can determine how we fare in life, how we deal with others and how they can relate to us.

In the same way as you looked up to someone important in your life and used trying to emulate some of their traits as an attempt to discover yourself, so your child is doing the same. Some of the things you do might attract them and others might put them off completely, but be under no illusion: they are watching. And if you are showing them that you are not worthy of care and focus, at a subconscious level, it will become the de facto position.

The way you behave towards yourself, the language you use, the actions you take and the priority you give yourself, can also impact on how your child sees you and how they see themselves. It gives them permission to treat you in a certain way. This may be good or bad, but if you are not taking care of you and realising your own value and worth, why would you expect them to?

Lightening the load

It is essential that your child isn't left with the feeling that their illness is a drain on you. I'm not suggesting you gloss over how you feel or paint a smile on and pretend that everything is OK. It's important to recognise and acknowledge the illness, but your child really doesn't need the extra weight of the guilt that they're ruining your life by being ill. If you aren't taking care of yourself, it can feel to your child that they are a burden. Your family life may have changed beyond recognition. Where once there were jobs and school and holidays and hope, that might all be on hold. If you can't maintain a sense that you matter despite that, it will make it hard for your child to not feel they are the root cause of the changes in you.

Making a Plan

Self-care needs a plan if we're going to make it a part of how we greet this extraordinary time and get through it in one piece. We have to try to make self-care part of our routine if we're going to build on it and benefit from it, so understanding what it means to us can make it more likely we'll stay the self-care course.

Step 1: Permission and commitment

Self-care starts when we give ourselves permission to nurture ourselves. If you haven't already, give yourself permission now to take care of yourself. Permission, backed by commitment, can help us to bring about really potent change in our lives. Commitment is about committing to ourselves and knowing that we're worthy of self-care. And if that's tough for you to do, then commit to self-care for your child, so you can be a better parent to them.

Commitment can get tripped up if we hold negative views about ourselves. Maybe you think you'll make mistakes, expect yourself to be able to change overnight or judge yourself harshly about something that should be nurturing. Many of these beliefs will be gently challenged and broken down by self-care, but it will take time.

Step 2: Your self-care 'essentials'

Get yourself a pen and paper, or open a note on your phone, and let's make your plan. What are the 'essentials' your body and mind need to feel its calmest, best self? What does your sense of peace miss if you don't do it? It could be that you find yourself grouchy on anything less than eight hours sleep. You might really need a weekly chat with a friend. It could be that your morning run or yoga on YouTube is non-negotiable. Maybe drinking less than two litres of water impacts on your mood. Write them down.

Not sure what your essentials are? Take a look at your routine and monitor it for a week. What parts of it work well for you? What things do you miss if you don't find time to do them? Make a note of these.

Look at the human essentials we have: sleep, water, food, light, movement, connection. Mark yourself out of 10. How are you doing? Are there any quick wins or small changes you can make to get more of what you need?

Step 3: Your self-care 'superchargers'

These are the things that make you feel great! Write a list of things you like to do, that make you feel good and that give you a sense of comfort. It might be reading a novel, playing Candy Crush, eating chocolate, belting out Barbra Streisand while driving, looking at photos. List as many things as you can.

Don't be shy to add things you haven't done before. If it sparks a sense of excitement in you, write it down. Say yes to horse riding, trying archery or learning how to make baked Alaska. Some of them might not be possible right now, but this is about reconnecting with your 'self' and understanding what lights you up. Pottery was on my list for a long time and became a cornerstone of my self-care. Horse riding is something I love to do, but I haven't found a way to do that yet. And that's OK. Planning a trek to Montana that may never come off is as much self-care as actually going.

If this is hard because you've never really thought about what makes you happy, remember the things you used to love, before life got in the way or someone made you question it. Simple pleasures – a hot water bottle, the scent of a candle, putting on fluffy slippers – things that make you *feel* are also great ways to start self-caring.

Your self-care essentials and superchargers are what you can lean on when you need self-care. To complete your plan, try to schedule something from the essentials list several times a week, and something from the superchargers list every week. Start small and build up. Having things that support your self-care close to hand helps making this priority part of your routine.

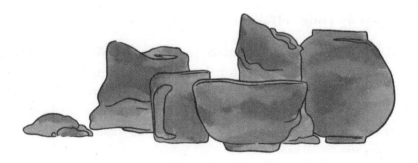

How do you self-care?

Real self-care is about nurturing ourselves, not berating ourselves for having a brownie. Yes, it is eating well, because that keeps us healthy. It is exercising, because our bodies are built to move and reward us with chemical rushes when we do. It is going to bed at a reasonable hour because sleep is such a powerful boost for us.

You prioritise the things that help to keep you in optimum health and well-being. You get curious about what comforts you and what lights you up, and you commit to keeping it up, even if it's only for a snatched moment in the day.

It might also be belly laughing with your partner, staying up late to chat to a friend, eating a whole bar of chocolate, crocheting or planning a trip on Pinterest. It's the things that nurture you positively now and for your future.

Self-care might also be a whole load of things that you might not think of:

- Saying no to obligation or an invitation.
- Saying yes to help and support.
- Saying not today.
- Having a takeaway when you'd planned to cook. Or cooking from scratch if you enjoy it.
- Sleeping in the afternoon without guilt.
- Standing barefoot on the grass.
- Drinking a refreshing glass of water.
- Paying bills.
- Organising your wardrobe.
- Remembering good times.

Your self-care list is such a personal thing. My self-care might be your worst nightmare, and vice versa!

I don't have the time or space to self-care!

You may feel, as I did, that taking time out is impossible because you're on high alert, waiting for the next explosion, suicide attempt, self-harming or fallout from a therapy session. Maybe you're juggling challenging work and relationships in addition to your child's mental health issues. When is there any time for you? You need more resources than you have available and so you look at self-care, or taking care of yourself, as a waste of energy. At times, it can even feel like an act of disloyalty to your child, as if you're placing your needs above theirs.

It may be that each time you've put on your gym gear, or arranged to meet a friend for a coffee and a catch-up, or bought some ingredients to make a beautiful healthy dinner, or just sat down with your eyes closed for a few moments, you've found that it's the exact time your child needs you. Maybe, like I was, you're using less than healthy methods of coping. It's OK.

There are ways you can weave self-care into your day that take into account the importance of your role as a parent. Maybe it's listening to a podcast and not the news in the car as you drive to a medical appointment and your child has their headphones in. Maybe it's making sure you take a book or magazine for the waiting room. Maybe it's getting up just 10 minutes earlier to enjoy a quiet cup of coffee. Creating a space for your self-care can help – maybe it's your bedroom or the bathroom. Maybe it's a figurative space, so when your family is settled, however much ironing is piling up, that's your self-care time. It is a practice and it takes time to build, but you are helping everyone by starting.

Gift yourself 10 minutes where you can step outside and feel the elements on your face. If that's too much, ask someone for a hug or give yourself one, or go and wash your hands and rub in some hand cream. I used to make myself sit down at 9.20am every weekday morning, alone, in peace, with a cup of tea to listen mindfully to 'Pause for Thought' on Radio 2. If we had an appointment, I'd try to listen in the car and, if that didn't work, I'd find some time in the day to listen again on the app and carve out that precious 10 minutes of contemplative time for myself. In time it became a ritual. I started to really value that time and to consider ways I could ensure it was a time of nurture for me. I bought myself a special morning mug and special teas to try, and that 10 minutes became my oasis. I started to consider the impact of this 10-minute ritual. It made me stop, it made me consider myself in all of the chaos and it made me feel connected, if only by passive means. This was all I could do at the time, but it meant a lot to me. No one else knew about it. No one needed to. You can find something that's yours, a routine that becomes a ritual, without anyone ever knowing.

How to Nurture You

Self-care isn't the latest avocado-filled fad or someone else's suggestion (though it might be!). It's an act for the self and the soul, and is unique to you. Most of all, self-care isn't selfish. It's not a sign of emotional weakness or something to be ashamed of. It's not only for those who have the time and resources to dive into it, it's something that we all need and deserve, and we can give it to ourselves every single day. An easy place to start is by carving out 10 minutes for yourself and telling yourself that you matter.

Take time out

Taking time out is important if you're going to make it through this experience in one piece. It's often about an escape from a moment or a feeling, rather than a place. How can you find the time and space that gives you some respite and reprieve from the chatter and concern? You start small.

We all have 10 minutes, and we can find it every single day. However busy you are, however worried, tormented or tired, it is your resistance around finding that time that is the problem; resistance to being important, saying you're worthy, standing up for you first – these are the things that stop you from listening to your needs. Schedule that time and allow yourself to fall head first into it. Every time you do it, it becomes easier.

Finding my place of calm

I stumbled upon the kind of calm I needed when I found Kara, potter extraordinaire, in a little studio in the village I live in. A wonderfully calm and creative woman filled with peace and grace, she allowed me to potter around (literally) with clay. No pressure, she held space for me each week. Sometimes I sobbed, sometimes I rambled, sometimes I mastered the wheel, and other times I sat making patterns, rolling out clay tiles and tidying her pots of glazes. By the time the three hours were up, I had expelled the build-up of emotion and could return to my life with a renewed sense of my own capabilities. Sadly, my capabilities were not hugely creative, but it didn't matter; I love the pots I made. They signify a time when I was seeking validation and connection with myself and I found it through a bag of clay.

Find calm in nature

Another place of calm for me was walking in the fields around my house. Things are always growing and changing and becoming in nature, and spending time in nature seems to challenge the pause that has been placed on our own lives.

The natural world seems to offer a hope that only something that has existed beyond our comprehension can. Getting outside is great because of the fresh air, the exercise and the vitamin D. It is also an opportunity to get out all your frustration among some space, away from your family. I am sure I cut a strange figure against the brown and then green of the changing fields, stamping my feet, yelling at the top of my voice and throwing my arms in the air in exasperation at not being able to change things. But I felt better for it!

Gratitude

This is the act of noticing, and perhaps writing down, the things that you are grateful for. It can be a little thing, such as a nice breakfast, or something much bigger. I came late to the benefits of 'gratitude'. I think I've always been a person who is thankful but I'm not sure I was actively grateful until I joined in a challenge on Facebook where I had to share three things I was grateful for every day for five days. By actively, consciously identifying the things I was grateful for, the pleasure and delight around them lasted longer and became a source of joy that I could tap into at any point I needed a boost. Nothing in my life had changed, but I was able to find more joy in the smallest things.

There are hundreds of scientific studies that show the benefits of a daily gratitude practice, and we now do it in the Parenting Mental Health group. Many of those who started the gratitude challenge report that it has improved their mood and outlook. The things around them haven't changed, but gratitude has changed how they see them.

By consciously recognising three things every day that bring you joy, you can literally rewire your brain. We can thank neuroplasticity (the brain's ability to change itself throughout our lifetime) for this. Neuroplasticity is the secret ingredient of gratitude, because each time you recognise something you're grateful for, it re-lays your neural pathways. Along with synaptic pruning, neuroplasticity helps to strengthen our positive neural connections and remove the ones that are no longer needed or useful. So gratitude not only changes your brain to help you to look for the positive, it also helps you to continue to find the good in whatever you're facing.

Gratitude impacts on our physical body too. According to research completed by Robert A. Emmons from the University of California and Michael E. McCullough from the University of Miami, keeping a gratitude journal led to 16 per cent fewer physical symptoms in those who took part and 10 per cent less physical pain. THNX4.org, an online gratitude journal set up by the Greater Good Science Center at the University of California, found that people who practised gratitude benefited from less stomach pain, better skin, fewer headaches and reduced blood pressure.

Emmons' and McCullough's paper, 'Counting blessings versus burdens', found that gratitude impacts on sleep, increasing sleep quality by 25 per cent and the amount of sleep by 8 per cent. Gratitude can even help you to exercise more. Participants in Emmons' and McCullough's research reported 19 per cent more time exercising. All from being grateful.

So how do you tap into the goodness of gratitude and benefit from its power? It's simple, it's easy and it's free. You commit to finding three or more things you're grateful for, for at least 21 days. That's all you need to do. The 21 days is important, because that is how long it takes our brain to change.

1. Give it a go (even if you are not sure you have time or it will work) – there is no harm in trying.
2. Go back to basics and try to find three things you're grateful for. It could be your ability to breathe, to walk around, to look outside. Some days are just too darned tough and you will find it beyond challenging to look past the noise in your head and the pain in your heart. Some days you look around and you simply can't be grateful for the details. At this time, if you want to try to help yourself, you have to be grateful for the basics.
3. Now try thinking of something special to you. Can you make it three things? If you like, make a note in a journal or just say them to yourself. Maybe you recognise your gratitudes as you go to bed, or maybe you find one in the morning, one at lunchtime and one in the evening. Or think of them on the loo, when you're boiling the kettle or brushing your teeth. Use it as a way to ground yourself when you're having a bad day (or life). Whatever works for you, just keep being grateful!

The daily gratitude

The 'daily gratitude' post in the Parenting Mental Health community has become an anchor for those of us who are feeling the benefits of gratitude. It's also a reminder to recognise the good, which is particularly useful when life gets busy or things improve. Join us in the Facebook group and try it out.

In my experience, gratitude seems to be turbocharged by sharing. There is something wonderfully connective in the act of being grateful and sharing with others, but there's something alchemic when you reflect on others' gratitude. Even if it's by simply reading their words and not engaging in them beyond that, it seems to fuel a deeper connection to the sense of gratitude we have.

NOTICE SIMPLE PLEASURES

Some parents, in the midst of the tough times, find it hard to find gratitude. Sometimes just noticing simple pleasures is enough. At the end of one day, I got into bed and let out that relieved groan as my body sank into the mattress and began to relax. Another day, as I wrapped myself in a warm towel after a shower, it brought me to my senses and I felt grateful for the warmth and being able to really feel the feeling. These kinds of experiences bring us back to the moment and remind us we are *feeling* beings at a time when we are numb and can't imagine feeling good again. Simple pleasures are a shortcut to gratitude. Some days when it feels all too much to be grateful for things, or when you say the words but begrudge them, simple pleasures come and take all of the obligation out of being grateful, because we just feel them. You can't be mad or sad when you're swept up in a moment. When you feel the warmth of the sun on your back, your body overrides your brain's rational thought. They are your path to gratitude.

Find a moment of stillness

There's a tree I can see from my kitchen window. I call it my tree (it doesn't belong to me, but that doesn't matter). We have a special connection. I watch it every day because it seems to take on changes in weather and season quickly, and it feels like a mini barometer for the world around me. It's also a beauty; a majestic, old oak that has been present through the generations.

As I made a cup of tea one morning, I found myself in a silent house. Aside from the fridge murmuring, there was no noise at all. With no urgency to get going and get out, I paused at the kitchen window and gazed out at 'my' tree: beautifully perfect and completely still. And that tree, coupled with the peace of the house, made me think about stillness, and the different types of stillness we have and need in our lives.

Stillness is an energy and a choice we bring to every day. Stillness can mean without motion or it can mean without thought. Whether it is a moment of stillness in meditation or a reflection of the way we face our lives, stillness is a personal and powerful state. It can be vast, lonely and overwhelming, or it can be close, intimate and supportive.

The stillness I felt looking out of my kitchen window is the kind I urge you to seek out on a daily basis. It's a personal stillness, something to be enjoyed rather than endured. Finding

a moment of stillness is a simple way to reground yourself when times are tough. Is there a moment in your day where you can find a little space for stillness?

Meditation

Meditation can help us to find a mental sense of calm and expansion that offers us space to feel and be present. This quote from Thich Nhat Hanh sums up the benefits of being mindful and present, both for us and our children: 'The most precious gift we can offer others is our presence. When mindfulness embraces those we love, they will bloom like flowers.'

According to the Nalanda Institute, meditation is 'a conscious exercise of attention, that builds our mind and brain's natural powers of well-being, resilience and compassion. It is a powerful tool to eliminate stress, to heal the body, mind, and brain, and to enhance our personal well-being and positive relationship with the world.'

Meditation can be another powerful anchor in our day and, like gratitude, is a practice. The occasional attempt at both may yield some benefits, but it's when we decide we're going to commit regularly that the magic happens. Having activities that we repeat daily and bring us calm and peace builds our resilience, which we really need at a time of chaos.

You might not have meditated before, but I expect you've felt the sense of calm when you daydream or become immersed in a beautiful piece of music. I find myself meditating when I'm having my hair washed at the hairdresser – my mind becomes clear of worries and thoughts and I focus on my breath and the water flowing through my hair. I am fully present and focused on that moment. This is all that meditation is – a sense of focused calm and peace. A mind free of thoughts.

There are several apps, such as Calm, Headspace or Happy Not Perfect, that guide you through simple meditations and they're a great way to try meditation. You can set your phone to remind you to practice every day if you like.

Set your intentions

Intentions are a simple way to remain as present as possible, to focus on the day while progressing towards a goal or state you've chosen. 'What ifs' are unwanted intruders and thieves of our joy and contentment, but if we remain mindful, grateful and present, we can feel in charge of the day.

In the Parenting Mental Health community, we set our intentions at the beginning of every new week. It's a way to be accountable and to create some boundaries when life feels like it's running away from us. On a Monday, I invite our members to take themselves off somewhere quiet, grab a brew and a notepad, and get comfy. Intentions come from a place of stillness, so take some deep breaths in and out. If you're struggling to quiet your mind, close your eyes and breathe more deeply. Let your thoughts flow through your head, and let them pass on. Now in the quiet of your mind, what are you called to be, do, create or feel this week?

Maybe it's to be more patient with your child. Maybe it's to be more patient with yourself. Maybe it's to decide more consciously because you're seeing the impact of reacting, rather than responding. Maybe it's to create an amazing cake or space to relax or opportunity to have a challenging conversation.

So many of us feel that we have no power to effect change or even to choose when our family is in turmoil. But, we do. And setting intentions, to expand and not berate ourselves, is a gentle reminder that we have a choice.

Give yourself time to find that stillness inside of you so you can become intentional about how you take care of yourself. Being intentional maximises self-care's benefits. Build it into your routine. Enjoy the peace and safe harbour it offers.

Self-care catalysts

Over time, you might develop an awareness of when you really need self-care. Maybe your mood dips after seeing a particular family member, or when you have to call school, or when you try to get your child to shower. Our brains remember that these events are stressful, and so the build-up can become as much of a problem as the event itself. These are catalysts for self-care. Being honest with yourself about how they make you feel gives you a positive opportunity for self-nurture and self-love.

For everything you have to do that fills you with dread, wrap it with self-care. If you dread the psychiatrist's appointment, go in prepared. Preparation is self-care. Plan in a treat for yourself afterwards; whether that's scheduling in an hour to sit in silence with a frothy coffee, or going to the gym or scheduling a massage, take these catalysts seriously.

Journaling for self-care

If you're feeling battle weary and wondering where you go from here, grab a pen and a notebook and write down what you've been through and where you want to go next. Writing a diary, or 'journaling', is really enlightening at any stage of the curve (see page 67), but, in recovery, it can become the thread that connects our experience to insight. It can really provide us with the kind of 'Aha!' moments that shine a light on what we really need.

Therapy

Would you tinker with your own car if it was broken or try to mend your boiler? I hope not, for safety's sake! You'd go and find someone who is trained and qualified to help you identify the problem, agree a course of remedial work and complete it safely. It's the same with your own mind.

'Therapy' is a blanket term for a number of disciplines, from CBT (cognitive behavioural therapy) and counselling to psychotherapy, and more. I urge you to consider getting some professional help for yourself as you navigate this time. Coming to terms with the loss of what we believed we had and facing an uncertain future has the makings of cognitive chaos. If we don't explore our feelings, they can become overwhelming, leading to us becoming mentally unbalanced.

If you're already having therapy or seeing a counsellor, I applaud you. I don't think therapy is anything to be ashamed of; in fact, I think standing up and recognising that you need help to move through a difficult time is a sign of strength.

Fortunately, our idea of therapy has moved from the old-fashioned perception of lying on a couch and speaking to someone who appears to have no connection with you, to an amazingly warm, creative and positive experience.

I see supporting a child through mental illness as a form of trauma. I didn't recognise this myself until Issy was in recovery. It was then that I looked back at the impact of the illness and knew we had all been through something powerful and life-changing.

Therapy can help you process what you are going through and also explore who you now are. It's so common to feel a sense of grief and loss of self and feel differently because of this experience. You might be wondering who you are because you were defined by being a parent and feel that you've failed in some way. You may be carrying a huge amount of baggage from your own childhood and find that facing this and making peace with it is necessary to help your family through this time. When we were asked by Issy's psychiatrist about our past and parenting approach in an attempt to check if we were making her ill (it's usual, there was no malice), the psychiatrist gave me some insight into my own childhood that was illuminating and life-changing. She suggested I had some psychotherapy, which really helped me to come to terms with things I hadn't been able to master alone with a pile of self-help books.

Sleep

'I love sleep. My life has the tendency to fall apart when I'm awake, you know?'

Ernest Hemingway

Sleep is not only an escape from your emotions, but it is like having your very own fuel-recharging system available. But sadly, at a time when you're overwhelmed, over-worried and in need of rest, sleep may elude you. Maybe you're lying awake listening to your child crash about at 4am. Maybe you can't stop the incessant thoughts flying around your head.

It's safe to say, we all feel better after a good night's rest. Stress, busy minds, lack of time and, for women of a certain age, a change in hormones, can all lead to not being able to get to sleep, waking up in the night or simply not getting enough.

In many ways we're mirroring our teenagers – stress, life choices and hormones are all things that impact on their sleep too, and while we get exasperated at their sleep schedules, maybe our own sleep schedule isn't doing us any favours either. A lack of sleep has an impact on the prefrontal cortex – this is where we make decisions and, without good sleep, it doesn't function well. We need to sleep well to make good decisions. If your child is struggling with sleep, which is such a common part of mental illness, and you're finding yourself awake comforting them in the small hours, listening to them chat to their online friends while gaming or you're simply unable to sleep for worry, you're not alone.

Sleep hygiene

This is the catch-all term for the things we have control of to give ourselves the best chance of a good night's rest. It isn't likely to be high on your list of priorities, but if you can make small changes to try to improve the quality and length of your sleep, you'll find that what you face doesn't feel quite as challenging. Good sleep comes when our minds are at peace, but it is also helped by a few practical changes:

- **Keep your bedroom dark.** Light plays a huge part in your ability to sleep well. That's why a 'no device' rule for an hour before bed is a good start. Exposure to light at night stimulates alertness, so keep your room dark to give your body the best shot at undisturbed sleep.

- **Clear the clutter.** Is your room filled with laundry, unread papers or things you need to mend? It's time to move them out. Having a space that is messy can lead to thoughts of unfinished tasks that disrupt our rest.
- **Clear your mind.** Put down your worries, your stresses and your phone. Take out a notebook and write down specifics that are concerning you, create a to-do list for today or write a note to yourself that you have permission to rest.
- **Consider the smell.** Open the windows and air the room. Use an essential oil in a pillow spray or diffuser. Lavender is known for its relaxing powers.

Positive Self-Talk

We all have an inner voice, and how we use it to speak to ourselves both in our heads and out loud informs the way we think of ourselves. It also influences how we present ourselves to the world, including our family, and how the world responds to us. How you talk about yourself informs your child on how to perceive us and how we perceive ourselves, and it lays down the blueprint for how our child sees their own value too. It also impacts on relationships with partners, colleagues, clients, family and friends. It's a barometer of what we'll allow.

I've learned from years of self-worth and self-esteem issues just how potent positive self-talk can be as a mechanism to keep your spirits up, give yourself a break and positively impact on your child's mental health.

If you tell yourself you're incapable, undeserving or that things will never change, your inner script will reinforce this negativity and start to impact on your actions so you make real what you think and believe.

Removing negative self-talk can feel like a mountain to climb, particularly if it's been your language of choice for some time, but there are some simple ways we can begin to change it. Being negative serves no positive purpose at a time when we need all the positive resources we can get our hands on. Decide now to try to talk more positively to yourself and about yourself. Changing that inner monologue is a practice, but, once it's happening, it frees us to shape a new narrative within ourselves.

A 2014 paper from the American Psychological Society says that if you use the third person ('he', 'she') in your self-talk instead of 'I', it helps you to regulate how you speak to yourself. It also takes some of the judgement and repetition of negativity away. By using the third person in self-talk, we can begin to step back and think more objectively about our responses and emotions. It can help us to stop turning over old events and situations in our mind.

You can also give your negative self-talk a name. Mine is 'Brenda' or 'Mavis', depending on the day. Giving my negative inner voice a name means it's not a part of me – it's a rude old biddy, or a mind monkey, or a gremlin, as Brené Brown calls it. Trying to extract 'you' from these voices is a really positive step towards mental calmness. If I asked you to commit to kindness to a friend, I am sure you would not hesitate. So, let's give it a go!

Switching how to talk to yourself

Find yourself a notebook or open a note on your phone. You don't need to set aside a special time in the day, just notice things as they appear.

1. Start small. As you go about your day, notice some of the negative thoughts that pop into your head. Write down some of the things you say to yourself. Is it 'I got that wrong', 'I'm not good enough', etc.? Read them back. Would you say them to a friend? I doubt it.

2. Try to think of a way to replace the thought with some kind talk. Remind yourself of all the good things about yourself. If you don't know what to say to yourself to counter the harshness, just say, 'I am enough' or 'I am good'.

3. If you are not sure what your kind voice sounds like, why not use a friend's voice or a singer's or even Oprah's – someone who wouldn't dream of talking to you in a bad way.

Make some affirmations

Some time ago, I ran a workshop on mental health with a dear friend who is an amazing creative counsellor. As part of the day, she suggested we had some affirmations printed up to challenge the attendees' beliefs about themselves.

I took a set of these affirmations home and, after Issy had taken the ones she wanted, I was left with one card that ended up by my bed. It said: 'I am worthy of self-compassion and self-love.' I looked at this card every night before I went to sleep and each morning when I woke up. I thought to myself, 'of course I am'.

But something inside niggled at me. Did I really, truly, deeply feel that?

As the days passed, something started to shift. The card became a siren, calling out to me and challenging me to believe it, and challenging me to challenge why I didn't or couldn't believe it at times. I found myself pondering on the feelings I got from reading it as I drifted off to sleep. I woke up and started to read it with more vigour and verve. In a short space of time, I started to actually believe it. I *was* worthy of self-compassion and self-love!

I felt a shift to believe something different about myself from reading and rereading those words; words that I would never have told myself on a daily basis had they not been printed up on a lovely card. And those words and that belief are the catalyst we all need to shift our thinking towards a more compassionate and loving approach to ourselves.

Why not try this one for yourself? Find a lovely piece of card and a favourite pen. Some positive affirmations you might use on your card could be:

- 'I take care of my family when I take care of myself.'
- 'I treat myself with the compassion and care I give my family.'
- 'I deserve to be loved and nurtured.'

Place your card where you can see it every day. And, in time, I hope that you will believe it too.

Life Beyond Mental Illness

While self-care during crisis is about having the strength to carry on in the everyday, as your child begins to recover, self-care is also about rebuilding your own resilience and reserves. It is also important to heal the wounds that this experience has created and to make you who you need to be to reconcile with this experience.

As your child starts to improve, it can be hard to determine when they're ready for you to change the routine and you're able to move some of the focus away from them. As long as your child is safe, the time is *always* right to explore your needs and engage in some self-care. 'Building your resilience' means allowing yourself to let your child do things without you hovering around them. It means setting aside your fears and believing in possibility. It means recognising your needs and understanding how you've met some and not others during this time.

Taking care of ourselves helps us to reach beyond the moment, to dream of a time beyond today and to hold the belief that we will come through this. So, how do we retain the drive and impetus to look after ourselves on a regular basis? To continue to be kind when it's easier to fall back into old, familiar yet uncomfortable habits?

If slow and steady wins the race, little and often makes the change. Don't give up if you have a bad day with your self-care, sleep or outdoor exercise. Don't beat yourself up if you're impatient or your fear comes out in a growl. Be kind to yourself if all you manage to do today is cry yourself dry. The best antidote to all of these states is being kind.

Keep in mind . . .

1. If starting this journey to nurture yourself feels too difficult for you, start small. Notice when you are being harsh to yourself and stop. Have a few minutes extra in the shower, guilt-free. Find small ways to nurture yourself, every day.

2. If it feels too difficult to do self-care for you, do it for your child. Remember that you are the blueprint for your child and they are watching. You're not likely to see the impact on them of being kind to yourself

right away, but, in time, your child will replay your self-kindness in the way they treat themselves and others. Start it for them, stick at it for you.

3. For many of us, speaking to ourselves with warmth and grace, showing ourselves compassion and getting on the list and remaining a priority in our lives are acts of bravery, particularly at a time where we feel our priority shouldn't be us. I know how hard this can be. Keep going. You're absolutely worth it.

10

You and Your Partner

'Love does not consist of gazing at each other, but in looking outward together in the same direction.'

Antoine de Saint-Exupéry, *Airman's Odyssey*

If you have a partner, your child's mental health journey can place untold pressure on your relationship. Maybe you disagree on how best to deal with it. Maybe one of you thinks like a partner (see page 179) while the other feels your child is manipulating the situation. In this chapter, we'll cover how you can try to stay connected through this time.

When your child is experiencing symptoms of a mental health disorder, everything else in your life becomes less important and all your energy is compelled to make things better. All thoughts of how your partner might be feeling, the small considerations that lift your interactions and maintain connection, and even the importance of your relationship, are generally swept aside.

This lack of connection can very quickly lead to resentment and isolation and, at a time when you need to pull together, to be supported and nurtured, there can be a real disconnect that not only harms you, but can harm your partner and your child too.

'It's seriously tested our relationship. We come at it from two different ends of the spectrum. One emotional, openly caring and affectionate. The other comes across grumpy, robotic, lacking empathy for our child and the impacts on me. This has caused so much tension, unhappiness and rows. It even got to a low point when I said it was over between us if the behaviour continued. I wasn't going to stand back and watch the behaviour going on.'

S, parent of 16-year-old

I'm no relationship therapist, in fact I'm no therapist at all, but I know from experience that when your child is ill, the state of your relationship changes because of the pressure that uncertainty brings. However close you've been, there can seem to be simply no space for intimacy and your relationship can take a backseat as you fight to understand this new normal.

When you've been battling for recovery for a long time, your relationship can end up as a platonic afterthought and, if you're not careful, over time it can turn into an annoyance. Considering how your partner feels and their needs can become a burden. Generally it's not because you don't love them; it's because all your brain wants to do is to solve the main problem. It doesn't want to be romantic. It doesn't want to listen to the issues with Bob at the office. And it really doesn't need to be told how to do the job in hand better. It doesn't have the patience to filter and understand the true intention of your partner's words. Your brain has a big problem to solve and it will pump all necessary energy towards that.

Being a carer is exhausting and often doesn't give you room

to nurture a relationship with yourself, let alone someone else, or to see yourself as a person with needs and desires and a right to them. So if you don't feel you're on the same team, it can become a burden that none of us need or deserve.

Wherever you are in the curve (see page 67), the important thing to recognise is that you and your partner don't have the same experiences and expectations, and will approach this situation differently.

The roles you play in the relationship can be amplified – if your child's practical day-to-day welfare is your domain, then your partner may expect you to have all the answers, and questions born of fear about what on earth is happening can feel accusative and harsh.

A united front is critical to not add to your child's burden. Whether they vocalise it or not, your child will already be feeling that their circumstances are a negative, so if they see you're not together and you're rowing about elements of your life that relate to your child, it can be destructive.

Managing Different Parenting Styles

Differing parenting approaches, ones that you probably didn't support before your child became ill, are suddenly magnified. Fighting over whose approach is right can become the same old, same old conversation.

Respecting your differences can be hard when your partner's actions seem to go completely against the goal you're meant to share: support and care for your child. Maybe they don't see your child's illness and shout and punish it as if it's bad behaviour. Or they demand that things remain exactly as they like them, whatever the impact on your child or you as a family. I know that is a tough situation to face: I've supported a large number of parents through this and there's no easy or quick fix. There needs to be a commitment on both sides, which can be hard to get to when all you can think of is your child and what their needs are.

But if you can really pull together, you may find that your relationship becomes something better than it ever could without these circumstances. Micro differences are magnified when you're fighting for sense and self, so if you are not aligned in your approach, the impact will be far greater and run far deeper than is helpful. A united front is best for everyone and, if you really mean it, it is even more powerful and won't result in more stress for you.

Here are some of the ways in which you can have a relationship that isn't overshadowed by your child's illness:

- Agree a common approach to your common goal.
- Decide what your core family 'goal' is. Ours is for our children to be happy, healthy and purposeful.
- Decide together with your partner that you're both on the same side and that this is a fight with mental illness, not each other.
- Reflect on the situations that can be stressful. Maybe it's an untidy room or that your child isn't washing as much as usual. Unpicking why this is such a flashpoint for either of you can help you to understand each other's viewpoint.
- Keep the communication open. What is your partner really saying to you when they rant and rave about your child and the situation you face? Angry and curt can translate to, 'I'm completely out of my depth. I'm terrified. I'm stressed.'

Sometimes parenting won't be fair

Sometimes you have to look beyond the fairy-tale hopes we all have of marriage and relationships and just suck it up. Sorry! You might have to be the responsible one for a while to keep this relationship on track and to keep the communication open and productive. You may have to do more of the heavy lifting to keep everything moving forward. And I know that feels unfair. I told you earlier that this experience has the power to change you; it also has the power to transform your relationships.

Partner Your Partner

Partnering is a shift in communication and behaviour that can work well with your child, so why not try it on your partner too? It's simple, it's free and it's kind. While they may wonder what you want at first, over time partnering enables loving, close relationships. It doesn't happen overnight, but by looking beyond what they *should* be doing for you and responding kindly, empathetically and generously to your partner, you can both come through and feel good, and your child will pick up on the positive vibrations. Having parents who are respectful of each other and loving towards each other (even if they're not together) is a gift you can give your child. It shows them how to have a positive relationship, how to navigate adversity and challenge, and that their illness hasn't ruined something else. It can often feel for them that they're the cause of all the disharmony in the home and, by trying hard to find the positive in your relationship, you'll also be helping your child.

'*I accessed therapy through work insurance to deal with my issues with my daughter, but ended up mostly talking about my husband and the resentment I felt (a lot of "poor me" conversations). I was helped to realise that he was still there so I started saying what I wanted and how important he and the marriage were to me. It helped me stop the blame as he always felt guilty for how our daughter was and thought it was because of him. I used some of the partnering methods of "walking beside" him and "stopping fixing". The change has been phenomenal! He's the open, sweet man I married 23 years ago and we are going from strength to strength – he is mirroring my love, words and actions … just by me adding kindness and removing blame and resentment. He was there after all!*

'*I'm the happiest I've ever been in my marriage.*'

J, parent of 20-year-old

Making the effort

I hear you when you ask why should it be *you* making all the effort. But if neither of you makes the effort, then what will happen? Relationships take time, energy and commitment. If something is bothering you, then take the problem in hand and make the effort. What does 'make the effort' mean? It's about finding things that you can share together, taking care of yourself, being the best kind of you and keeping your energy levels topped up so you can be open and receptive to your partner. It means doing something small that makes a difference, such as picking up a copy of their favourite magazine, taking the dog for a walk so they can have a lie-in, letting them watch the football or *Strictly* – whatever they love – and being there for them or giving them space. If you see your partner struggling, give them a hug or suggest they head off to meet a friend or do something they like.

> 'Communication is vital. It took a year or two to be working on the same page. We also found that, even though we couldn't go on family holidays or leave the house at all, I encouraged my husband to go away alone, which really helped him recharge, which benefited me and my daughter. I find passing on therapist emails to my husband to read at his own leisure is helpful. I often talk about all the other families in similar situations.
>
> 'Cooking a nice meal and making the dining room a little romantic made sure we had time for us, but at home where I needed to be for my daughter. Sending texts helps us as, of course, he's not a mind reader and, when we are the ones coping 24/7, we can't expect them to know everything.'
>
> T, parent of 16-year-old

What About Me?

I know that all of this is lovely in principle, but it can leave you wanting to scream 'What about me?' If you're not being filled up, it's really tough to keep being the giver. Which brings me to the next point: Tell them what you need, tell them what you feel.

Maybe you need your partner to stop reacting a certain way when your child does something. Maybe you need them to show that they understand the pressure on you. Maybe you need more practical help – ask them to make dinner once a week or pick up the prescription from the pharmacy.

Maybe you need more emotional support; maybe you need them to take time off to come with you to appointments or to deal with school. Maybe for you it's about being hugged or kissed or made to feel special, or explaining your reluctance to have sex is due to stress, not that you don't find them attractive anymore. Maybe you need them to stop talking *at* you for a bit and to listen more. Or maybe it's about giving you a regular break. Whatever you need, share it with them. All this can get lost in trying to keep everything going. I know it's hard, but if you don't tell them what you need, they'll never have the chance to give it to you. If you don't ask, the answer is always no.

Easing the way to conversation

It can be tricky to ask for what you want or need. Here are some ways to start these sometimes awkward conversations:

- 'I feel . . . sad, anxious, worried, disconnected.'
- 'I'm concerned that/about . . .'
- Use sentences starting with 'I' rather than 'you'. Make it about your fears, not their behaviour.

Be assertive, be clear. Your partner isn't a mind reader. Even though they know you like no other, expecting them to recognise you're exhausted, in need of support and about to have a 'moment' can place a burden of expectation on them that neither of you need to deal with.

- If you're tired, say so.
- If you're in need of support, ask.
- If you're scared, share it.

- If you're in need of reassurance, reach out.
- If you're not sure if you can carry on, hand over the reins for a while.

Showing your vulnerability

How do you deal with stress? Are you a shouter or a sharer? Do you wear your heart on your sleeve or pretend things aren't happening? I know that when I am anxious and afraid, I isolate myself and make it hard for people to get in. However you deal with all of this stress, it's fine. That's your way. But by being vulnerable and sharing your fears with your partner, you open up a possibility for them to understand you better, enabling them to connect with you. You also make it OK to not be OK. So many times we try to hold things in because we're worried about the impact of letting it out on others. How about instead we face our truths and speak them out loud? How about we see them as powerful and transformative, rather than shameful and needy? Maybe sharing how you're *really* feeling will give your partner permission to share their fears too. And if two heads are better than one, two hearts are even more powerful.

Remembering all the good times

When we're faced with difficult times, we can begin to see traits we don't particularly like in people we love. It can be unconscious, as a way to try to pass blame or responsibility. At a time of enormous challenge, we can find our worst traits being highlighted. So, if there's no tenderness in your fingertips, think back to a time before mental illness and all the happy times you've shared. What made you fall in love with your partner? What are their best qualities? What good times have you shared? When did you think they were 'the one'? Take some time together to look through photo albums, to talk about favourite holidays and days out, for example.

Release the tension

Carrying around the intense panic of what was happening to my family as my daughter's mental health deteriorated, I felt as if my head was just one word away from exploding. Holding on to tension isn't good for us, and it doesn't make for a harmonious relationship.

Find ways to release the tension, whether that's by talking to yourself on a walk, writing your thoughts down in a journal (see page 51), telling a friend, venting in the Parenting Mental Health community (see page 54) or taking your fury out on the gym, some dough or the housework, it's important that you do it. Our partners weren't made to fulfil every need in us, so don't feel bad that you want to let things out to other people. It's healthy to let the tension go.

Incorporating relaxation, meditation (see page 162) and breathing exercises into your life can help you manage acute stress that comes from holding everything in. Try to let it out before it becomes a thing. Because you don't need something else to worry about.

Pace yourself

Marriage is the ultimate marathon and, whether you've got the piece of paper or not, your goal is a lifelong partnership. It does need regular energy, tending and attention to keep it going. But sometimes you can put it to one side, just for a while, if it feels like a fight and you don't have the capacity right now.

What If You Disagree?

It can be really hard sometimes to see the other person's point of view. We intrinsically believe that we're right. Before you get to the stage where you're 'shown' to be wrong, why not check in and see if any of your expectations or demands are causing issues with your partner. Perhaps you need to let go of some of the things that you hold on tightly to? You could ask your partner to share their views or you could consider a time when you and your partner were not in agreement – what caused this? Is there something you can change in your approach? What can you let go for a more harmonious life? I'm not suggesting this is forever, and you may not feel you can let go of certain things, but checking if there's an alternative can open up a range of conversations.

Maybe you feel it's your partner who needs to understand the impact of their actions on your child. Without breaching confidences, we can sympathetically and compassionately share how we see their words or responses make our child feel. Here are some ideas to help this go smoothly:

- The number one rule of this approach is: Don't feedback in anger. Start from a place of compassion. Being angry reduces your judgement and focuses you only on the negative. You can't take harsh words back and, if you approach this with any hint of anger or blame, it can potentially cause a bigger issue than the ones you want to broach.
- Choose a calm time to discuss any disagreements. Before bed when you are both exhausted isn't the best time, and neither is five minutes before you're due to leave the house. If your partner isn't in a place where they want to engage, it's probably not going to end well, so pause and wait for another time.

- Decide before you speak what you want to say. What are you trying to change? This isn't a slanging match or about making yourself feel better by making them feel worse. It's about effecting some change in the way they interact with your child and forging a stronger bond.
- Don't use the words 'always' and 'never'. When our brain can't engage its rational side, it can throw out generalisms in an attempt to make a point. It fails, and it hurts the other person.
- Be prepared to listen to what your partner says. They may feel angry at being 'accused' of something that is hurting their child. I doubt there's anyone reading this book who would want to, or consciously set out to, do that. Active listening can be really helpful here (see page 134).
- Finally, end it with a hug. Hugs in our house are the ultimate form of communication. It might be something else in your house. Whatever it is, do that. Move on. Look outward together.

Finding the positives

When I want to give feedback, I try to find something positive for every one thing that might be seen as potentially negative. Including things that you don't do well, or are also complicit in, can make it feel less like a trial and more like a positive and productive chat that forwards the family, rather than condemns one of you.

Share how grateful you are to your partner for the support and care they give to your child and the family. Find something good to say, even if you're cross at their lack of support.

Talk to friends

Though it's always good to talk, a word of caution here. Friends only know our version of events and, while it's great to offload to your friends, the best ones will know that it's not their place to judge or overlay their experiences on yours. Only you know what really goes on in your marriage or relationship, and only you can say what is acceptable or unacceptable behaviour.

Know that this is an extraordinary time and your relationship is unlikely to get as much of the focus and input that it really needs to thrive. It won't be perfect. But nothing is. Just don't let other people's expectations of it drive your actions. Make sure you do what you feel to be right for you and your family.

Schedule child-free time

I understand that it might not be top of your priorities, or you may think it's impossible, but spending time alone away from your child, whether that's out of the house or not, is important. It can be all-consuming to be Mum or Dad the whole time. When are you 'you'? And when are you an adult in a relationship? The answer is when you make the time to be. Whether it's a date night, a simple trip out to collect the groceries, a date on the sofa with a film or a romantic meal for two in your kitchen, try to see this as an essential part of your child's recovery and your family's resilience. Find ways to sneak in time together, alone. Maybe it's by tagging along when your partner goes out to collect something. Maybe it's by enlisting the help of grandparents, friends or neighbours and planning a night out, or even a night away.

'We schedule regular time for us – yes! As if work and life weren't busy and demanding enough: dealing with a child with mental health issues, the school, the medical support, the upsets, it's like a fog that descends over your relationship and it's so easy to lose your way. We have at least one "date" a week. We try to have any serious conversations beforehand; if we're down or fed up and worried about our daughter, we both make an effort to be cheerful and positive when we go out.'

J, parent of 18-year-old

Learn to compromise

Compromise can feel, well, compromising; like we're giving more than we're getting. But if we see love as an infinite game, where we play to stay in the game, it can feel good to set aside our needs and make the adjustments that allow our relationship to continue to work, and even flourish. If it feels like hard work, do it for your child rather than your partner. Remember what your core family goal is (see page 178). Would your compromise move you closer to that? At what cost to you?

But what if you've done all the giving and still reached stalemate? When you've nothing left to give, then what?

When to seek help

Sometimes the challenges of parenting a young person with a mental illness can be too great for us to resolve alone, and there's strength in recognising our need for external help. While we can urge our children to see professionals to resolve their challenges, we can overlook our own need for some specialist support. You have two options: going to a therapist together or alone.

If your partner is open to couples' therapy or counselling, fantastic! You may feel it signifies the beginning of the end, but it is, in fact, the start of a whole new relationship between you. Aside from the impact of mental illness on our relationships, we are likely at a stage in our lives when we're questioning ourselves, our worth and our place. Why not build your relationship to meet both your changing needs?

Going to a therapist alone, for yourself, can help your relationship because, although it may sound clichéd, you can't love someone else until you love yourself. Give yourself that gift of space to explore how you're feeling. It's an act of self-love to stand up and say you need support. You deserve it; your relationship deserves it; your family deserves it.

Managing Feelings of Guilt

But what if you feel that being connected to your partner when your child needs you is wrong? What if you feel guilty for having that connection when your child is ill? We have a number of relationships in our lives and a number of ways of loving. And as amazing infinite humans, we have the capacity to love in many different ways. We can love our children, friends, partners and ourselves, all at the same time.

The relationships we aim to cultivate with our children are some of the most important we will have the privilege to create. But they are not the only relationships in our lives, and we have to balance what we put into our children with our needs and those of the wider family. Sometimes that means we compromise, finding ourselves in relationships that don't enrich us, or reacting in a way that goes against our principles so we can keep the peace while we seek out our bravery. Sometimes that means we choose ourselves, just for a day, or an hour, or 10 minutes, and that sends a powerful message to our children about how we value ourselves.

Whatever way you get through is *your* way; it is your choice and your life. You deserve love, to give and receive it. Whatever relationships you choose to have, or not to have, during this time, it's your choice. But please, don't feel guilty for loving someone. Whether it's your child, your partner or yourself, you deserve to love and be loved.

Practical Ways to Connect

There are many ways you can invest in your relationship, even during these tough times. If you need a little inspiration, here are some ideas to try:

- Take on one of the chores your partner normally does.
- Share what you're feeling, openly and honestly (see page 182).
- Write love notes to your partner, sharing what you like about them.
- Text them a message when you're not together.
- Do something you know they'd like – download their favourite box set or cook their favourite meal.
- Recognise special anniversaries – with a card, a hug or a homemade picnic in the garden – whatever speaks to you and connects you both.
- If possible, book a night out or away together.
- Keep the physical connection going through hugs and kisses and holding hands even if sex is just too draining.
- Praise your partner to your child – don't put them down.

Mental illness brings a sea change for all involved and it is natural and normal for our relationships to change during this time. We're all made up of our experiences and look for others to fulfil needs within us, and mental illness doesn't tend to leave any room to give. Your child's mental illness may be a trigger for your partner's own experience that you're not aware of or you thought they'd overcome. It can feel like a very personal and individual fight, leading to withdrawal and a lack of connection. Your child's mental illness will impact on your relationship, but it doesn't have to be all negative. This is a chance to reconnect around what is important.

Keep in mind . . .

1. This is a challenging time for any partnership, but there is much you can do to help each other during this time.
2. Be clear with your frustrations – are you annoyed with your partner, yourself or the situation? Clear communication and a commitment to connection can transform how you navigate this time.
3. Invest in your partnership, whether through small things, such as helping each other out, or in seeking professional support. You are both worth it.

11

Friends, Family
and Mental Illness

As you read this book, wherever you and your family find yourself on the journey of mental illness, it's likely that you'll have had a moment when you looked around and felt completely, totally alone. Not only with the care of your child and all that entails, but in coping with the uncertainty that you face. You'll have realised that this illness has not only changed your life, but it has also changed your relationships with friends and family. One moment you were surrounded by calls and texts and connection, and then you blinked, and things changed.

Maybe it was a moment with a friend who changed the subject, a teacher who glossed over the severity of your child's mental illness or a family member whose questions to try to understand your child's mental illness left you feeling judged, not supported. Maybe you sat in a room full of people and realised they had no idea of what you were going through. They were worried about things that didn't matter so how could they grasp the enormity of what you face every day? In this chapter we will look at how relationships can change with family and friends, and how you can deal with the challenges of their lack of knowledge, empathy or experience.

When Others Don't Get It

If you've ever come away from seeing a friend or family member and left feeling that you're fighting this battle alone, I hear you. It's a big ask to expect family and friends to understand the challenges you're facing, but sometimes the helpful/not helpful comments and suggestions can leave you questioning everything you thought you knew about your friendships and relationships.

When we want and need the support and understanding of our family and friends we can find that they don't all seem to grasp the severity of the situation or the impact of what they say. People find it easy to go straight into 'fix' mode when they hear your child is mentally ill. To many it seems to be a simple case of 'pull yourself together' or that you're not being tough enough with discipline or boundaries. This reaction is usually driven from a place of fear, often of the unknown, and this can mean that someone bypasses the essentials of connection like genuine concern, compassion and empathy. A person may appear to have suddenly become a self-certified expert on medication, psychology or behaviour, so ignoring their queries around if you'd 'just' make your child do X or Y and everything would be fine can be a challenge. A lack of experience can make people try to simplify a hugely complex and highly personal situation with some throwaway suggestions, and we can feel that our justification needs to swiftly follow their judgement.

Other people's 'judgement' isolates us at a time when we need more connection, not less. I found that many of my relationships changed when my daughter was ill. For example, I didn't want to be around people who needed to question all the 'whys' and 'wherefores'. When we did manage to go out, I wanted a break from the pressure, not an interrogation about our rules and treatment. I wanted to escape into the detail and inanities of other people's lives, to hear about their jobs and their holidays and their hopes and their dreams, because, at that time, I didn't have these. I wanted to talk about normal things!

Preserving your energy

Caring for someone with a mental illness really does change you and your perspective, and that's OK. You may need to let go of, or redefine, some of the relationships that you have. Your finite resources are needed for the fight ahead. If people can't see from your responses that you're in need of support and not judgement, then maybe they aren't your people, or you may need space from them for a while. It doesn't mean that your relationship will be like this forever, but, for now, for your family's health and well-being, you need to focus on those who can walk alongside you or, at the very least, not make things worse.

How to deal with rudeness, judgement or indifference

Being a shield for your child is a key part of partnering (see page 86), and fielding unhelpful, judgemental and rude comments is hurtful and wearing to you and your child. You might want everyone to understand what is going on, but you're not on a quest to change or educate their minds. Your job is to support your child and yourself through their mental illness. You might encounter people who just don't get it – there might be collateral damage. You may have to come to terms with the loss of a friendship you thought strong enough to weather any storm. That's a challenge I know you won't want to face, but, like the challenges to your child's mental health, it's one that many of us have to take on. Maybe you will be able to refind those friendships another time.

Indifference is an easier 'fix'. You're in a fight for your child's future health and, in some cases, their life. You're simply too busy to worry about someone who doesn't 'get' it. Feel OK about letting that indifference wash over you. It doesn't make you a bad person, just one with a priority. You don't have the time, energy or capacity to educate or convert people who may not understand, so smile, nod and move on.

Rudeness can be found everywhere, but when it relates to your child who is battling an illness, it can be hard to overlook and may replay in your mind. Again, remember your focus and what your priority is. Don't engage. Answering back to rudeness or ignorance is only going to harm your sense of peace and probably won't change anything. Saying that, I don't expect you to wander around in a zen-like state of acceptance. That takes time and repeated practice. Venting is really useful (see page 54)!

Standing Alone

When Issy became ill, I found myself in a very strange place. We didn't belong to the world everyone else was living in. We stood alone. We fought alone. I cried alone. Standing alone is tough and challenging and not for the faint-hearted, but it does bring a sense of control that is otherwise lacking when you are dealing with mental illness. If you're alone, at least you don't have to deal with other people's assumptions and judgements, which often come from a strange mix of ignorance and love. Who knew that those two emotions could co-exist?

Having to be your usual bright and cheery self for other people's benefit when you're consumed with fear and worry is incredibly tiring, and it's something that I gave up quite quickly. Battling thoughts of if, how, why and when it will change compounds the isolation, leaving you locked in your own head. And that's the hardest part, isn't it? You don't want to be here in this situation. You don't want to be here for yourself, and you don't want to be here for your child.

With both friends and family, the lack of a common language means it is hard to communicate. Consider your situation. Maybe your child is unable to go to school and you're fighting a world that doesn't recognise their illness. Maybe your child is finding socialising an issue and you aren't able to see family every weekend like you used to. Maybe your beautiful child is in a psychiatric unit and you wonder what your family's future looks like.

Without experience of these situations, most people don't have the depth of understanding that allows them to be truly empathetic. The only words many seem to be able to draw upon are generalities that don't share the depth of emotion or confusion we feel. Generalities don't foster connection or understanding, and they can allow resentment and judgement to breed, leaving everyone feeling more isolated. Sympathy, a feeling of sorrow or pity, can feel judgemental when your child is mentally ill.

If friends and family 'get it', or not, let me reassure you that any judgement or misunderstanding is their problem, not yours. Mental illness is a big issue for people to grasp if they have no experience of it. And, let's be honest, they're busy with their own problems and they want an easy life. Being around mental illness is challenging. It feels infinite. There are no quick fixes or miracle cures.

When I drove around for six months with all our medications in my car boot to stop my daughter overdosing, I remember the bewildered look on a friend's face when I explained why. 'Can't you just tell her not to take them?' was a ridiculous thing to say to me while Issy was suicidal. It wasn't malicious, it was just a complete disconnect with the needs and pressures of her illness. And at a time when you're placing all your energy into supporting your child, it can feel like a stretch to be polite about such questions or to try to make other people understand the unique and bizarre experiences you are faced with. Often you might feel that it's for their benefit, and not yours, to do that.

If you have different views

You may find that suddenly you're seeing sides of friends you never expected to. Maybe they're dismissive of your child's symptoms, or they have strong views on antidepressants or certain treatments. If you've never had to personally face the choice of taking action in a situation – whether it's sticking up for your child in a school meeting, agreeing to your young teenager taking antidepressants or hearing them making themselves vomit after an overdose – it's easy to stick to the beliefs that define your sense of self and place. Don't waste your time on changing other people's opinions. You have more important work to complete.

Fear of judgement

I want to talk about how we can stop people connecting with us too. Many parents have spoken to me about a feeling of shame, of a fear of judgement. Shame stops us from articulating how we feel – *really* feel – and that stops others from having an opportunity to empathise with and support us. Shame silences us at a time when we need to speak clearer and louder than ever before and can isolate us from others. Maybe you feel ashamed of what you're going through. Maybe your friends and family are ashamed because they can't relate or effect any change.

I encourage you to be brave and see what you're going through as a huge lesson, not a judgement on your value as a person. Owning your story is something special, but it's scary because shame can be an easier, more familiar place to be. It's easy to blame ourselves and try to quieten the questions we find our brains asking us, relentlessly. But this doesn't help us, our children or our ability to connect with those around us.

Ways to Connect With Friends During This Time

Here are some ways to approach friendships in the time of mental illness. They won't 'fix' all your friendships, but they may help you find your people for this time in your life.

Be open with people

None of us are mind readers, so being as open about what you're facing as possible is essential in trying to build connection. How many times have you answered 'fine' when asked how you or your child are doing? Talking in generalities can be helpful as a self-preservation tool, but if you are seeking connection, it can hinder a personal exchange of understanding. Speak in generalities and you'll receive them back. 'Everything's fine' doesn't give anyone an opening to support you. Open your heart, if you can. Do it to the right people. You might think you know who they are, and you may be wrong. I was surprised where some of my strongest supporters came from. But if you come from a place of honesty, it can help you make sense and peace with what's happening, even if you don't get the response back that you are hoping for.

Park your assumptions

We all have different realities. It's hard to articulate how we're feeling about our child's illness to someone whose only worry is if their Amazon delivery will arrive before they have to leave for the school run. We've all been in that place and, while we know that a punctual delivery isn't really the only thing on their minds, it's easy to assume others have it much easier than you.

Maybe your friends don't understand because you've not fully shared what is going on. Maybe they're hurt that you haven't been around for them, because their lives have been challenging in different ways. They might not be dealing with a situation as all-consuming or potentially life-threatening as yours, but they will have their own concerns too.

It took me a long time to overcome my indignation about how some people treated us, particularly after our daughter came home from hospital. I have learned to realise that others also have challenges that appear as big and important to them at the time. Your challenge through this time is to connect with those who don't judge you and don't compare. Find the ones who are able to show empathy, compassion and kindness, especially when they don't understand what you're going through, and find time in their lives to listen and try to understand.

Lift and support

You may not feel it but you've been gifted an opportunity to reassess your life and that includes the energy of those involved in it. Who you associate with should lift you up and support you. They should want you to succeed and for your family to be strong. If they don't, let them go with love and peace.

Understand what you need

Some days you want and need a complete break from the life you're living, so finding a way to connect with your people, laugh, forget the pain and worry, and not be defined by being a carer, is really important. These are the days to hang out with your positive friends.

Some days you can be so angered by everyone else's positivity and perfect lives that it's safer to not go anywhere near a phone or laptop, or to engage with another human being.

Understanding that what you need can sometimes not be articulated because of the treacle in your head can lead you to a deeper acceptance of yourself and the limitations of others, and help you get through this time. It is your path to walk, and not everyone is able to join you on it, but you might find it highly therapeutic and really helpful to share with a trusted friend or lean into the comfort of your shared experiences and memories with them.

Prepare your story

Picture the scene. You find yourself opposite a friend, drinking coffee. It's a relief. You feel like a proper adult! You're out of the house, possibly not wearing pyjamas, and, for the first time in forever, the worries about your child are safely packaged up in a neat box that you've secured down with chains and rope. They're safe. It's OK. This is your time. And then the questions come: 'So, how are you? How are things?'

You need to be prepared. If things were 'normal' and mental illness not present, you'd be likely to chat about holiday/work/school, etc. But what do you do now? If you're going to meet a friend and don't want to feel you're being grilled or having to perform, or don't feel you can hold back the emotion, speak to them beforehand. A simple text to say, 'I'm really looking forward to seeing you. Things have been tough at home and I'd prefer not to discuss it today, so can you not ask me how I am? I'd love to hear all about what's going on with you but talking about our situation is hard at the moment.' The best of friends will understand that.

If you don't feel comfortable doing that, going with a 'story' really helps. Being prepared with a couple of sentences that give enough explanation but shut down further exploration can work well. This can give you the confidence to meet your friend without fear of breaking down or feeling a 'failure' when you say out loud what is going on in your life. Give some broad information and then ask a question, to take the onus away from you. An example might be: 'XX is doing OK at the moment. He's volunteering at the dog shelter and he enjoys it. How is XX getting on? Tell me about his trip.' Offer an opening for your friend to talk about something normal, so you don't feel compelled to reply with a detailed response that might bring you to tears and break down all your strength.

Let others partner you

Friendship is a two-way thing. I struggled at times to allow people to take care of me, because I thought our friendship was based on what I could give them, rather than what I brought by just being me. When you're in the throes of a crisis, desperately trying to understand where you are on this journey and how you are going to get through it, you can feel that you have nothing to give or bring.

Partnering is about walking beside someone while they go through an experience and accepting all they are and do. As a partner in someone's life, you don't have to have had the exact same experience. Who could you be partnered by? Who do you know who has the empathy, patience and love to help you through this time? You may find your partner is someone unexpected; your shared history might not be completely aligned, and you might wonder if and why they'd support you. I hope you can immediately think of a friend or family member who can partner you, but you might not feel you have anyone who could gift you that. You may feel you can't cope with your own feelings and don't want to burden someone else with them. You might feel that no one could want to be a part of your crazy, mixed up world. That's where new friends can help.

If you're struggling to find the kind of support you need from your existing circle of friends, maybe it's time to look outside of them and towards others in the same situation; check out online support or search for an in-person group (see page 55). You may end up being partnered by a whole community, and you're likely to find new friends who get it and get you.

'I am a qualified Integrative Counsellor, Therapeutic Stress Coach, author and mom to my 20-year-old autistic son who struggles with mental illness every day. He has post-traumatic stress disorder as a result of many years of bullying and has chosen to step out of life for now to heal and to recover. It wasn't that long ago that I was on "suicide watch", sitting on his bedroom floor crying my heart out into a pillow so that my son wouldn't hear me, while thinking that I'm just not a good enough parent. Wondering what I'm doing wrong. How is it possible that I *can help other people's children to be well but not my own? I was deeply hurting, and I felt powerless, alone and unable to find a way through!*

'In October 2018, I met Suzanne. I learned how her passion to educate parents about the importance of partnering vs parenting was a game changer for mental health globally and how her own experience of walking alongside her daughter through her mental illness was the inspiration for wanting to take on this incredible life mission to end generational mental illness. I soaked up all of her nuggets of wisdom and felt my beliefs shifting into a whole new way of seeing my son's mental illness, while helping me to release powerful emotions that I had swallowed so deep within me as a professional and as a parent. Through working with Suzanne, I have begun to heal my own story and my son is starting to find his way through too.'

Tanja Sharpe

It's OK to let go

There's a saying that I leaned on at times when I felt most alone: 'Friends are in your life for a reason, a season or a lifetime.' There is huge hope in this for me. It gave me permission to let go of people with love and peace (and, in some cases, a hefty slam of the door and good riddance) and not to hold on where it was clear they weren't aligned with where we were headed. Not everyone will make it through this time with you, and that's OK. Putting your time, efforts and energy into supporting your child means that you won't necessarily remember birthdays or important events, and you need to be surrounded by people who get that and understand.

This extraordinary experience will change you and it will change your tolerances for people. And that's OK too.

Family

There's an implied closeness and understanding that we all believe should be there in our family relationships: an understanding that we're doing our best, that we're conscious adults who don't intend to mess up and that we're not idiots. While friends are in your life by choice, it can be much harder to 'park' family or make peace with their judgements.

In some families, judgement is expected to be allowed and condoned. It stems from a hierarchical approach to parenting: 'I am right and not to be challenged. I have the right to express my views whether it is my place to or not.' If you were in any doubt about the benefits of partnering (see page 81), think of a time when you've been treated like a child and remember how disempowering and disconnecting it feels. Authority is judgement: the judger believes they are more right than the judgee. At this time in your life you need someone who walks beside you; not to fix you, not to get you to do what they think is right, but to truly empathise with what you're going through. You need people who can support you as *you* find the best way forward for you and your family, wherever that leads.

As I mentioned earlier, judgement comes from a place of fear. Your family may not understand the gravity of the situation that you are facing or they may be afraid of what the implications are for your child's future. Sadly, this doesn't always manifest in a positive way.

Expectations can lead to a breakdown in communication and connection. While you may have spent every weekend visiting your family or doing errands for them, you may find you have new priorities and plans may have to change. Maybe you've had to move your shift at work so you can make a medical appointment or you have a meeting at school you need to prepare for. Maybe you can't leave the house because you can't stop crying. Or, like I felt many times, the enormity of what you're going through is just so heavy, and complying with social cues and making polite conversation at a family special occasion is a weight you simply can't face.

Unless you're explicit, people won't realise that the connection between you may have changed. They're getting on with their lives and, unless told otherwise, they'll expect you to continue to deliver on what you've led them to expect from you up until now. They might not agree with the changes or understand them, but one thing you don't need to add to this situation is the expectation of others.

You generally can't see this from the outside in – you can only see the problem you need to resolve, which is how to help your child with their mental illness. Your family is probably not focused on that problem in the same way as you. If the situation with your child deteriorates, you may find they go into full-on fix mode where they try to simplify all the complexities of your child's illness into a to-do list to try to 'solve' it. They may demand you and your child 'just' do the things that seem so simple and obvious when you're not involved. They might dissect the past behaviour of your child or your parenting choices, as if your child is a science experiment and you're in need of educating. All of this, however helpful or harmful, generally comes from either a place of love and care, or a place of fear. Either way, it might not be what you need at this time and you can find yourself having a battle with people who are meant to be on your side. At a time where you're in need of support, having to rework the family dynamics is a project that you really don't want to get involved in. So how do you deal with it?

Forgive them

Forgiving your family for being human is a good starting point. It might feel like they don't deserve to be forgiven if they've made your child's illness into an issue, but holding on to the anger and resentment around this is not good for you or your child. It's hard to forgive someone for something said at your family's lowest point, but as someone wise once said, 'Holding on to anger is like drinking poison and expecting the other person to die.'

Let it go

You may just need to let a thoughtless comment go, rather than explain every single time. You may come to understand why they said what they did or you may not. It is unlikely they said it to harm you, although it can feel personal at the time. And it will take your precious time and attention away from your child, and from keeping you and your family on track. Park it until later and decide at some point in the future if it's still as important to resolve.

Forgive yourself

You would have gone to the birthday party if you could. There are times in our lives when we have to step away and recognise our own needs before others. Tell yourself now that it's OK to put yourself higher up the list. And if that feels hard, see it as a gift to your child.

Lower your expectations

Expecting family to step up and support us in the way we'd like can set us up for failure and disappointment and cause a wider rift at a time when none of us need any more drama. I know it's hard to conceive that your family won't understand what you're going through, but if you don't *expect* them to, you'll be pleasantly surprised if they do step up and support you. We don't all have the perfect family. In fact, *none* of us has the perfect family; there are always challenges and compromises, false memories and misunderstandings. While you can't control your family's beliefs and expectations of you, you can control your own beliefs and expectations. Being stoic about your family and the way they're dealing with your child's illness and the way they interact and support you can relieve some of the disappointment you may feel if you or your child are not given the treatment you expect. Expect the worst and you won't be disappointed. You are in control of yourself, and yourself alone.

You are not alone

There is a family of friends out there who get what you're going through and care about you and your life. I know, it seems incredible that someone you've never met could give you the kind of support you expect from those you thought were nearest and dearest to you, but they can. I see it every single day in the Parenting Mental Health community, and in many other groups and online communities.

Be explicit

Take a look at your conversations with your family and you'll probably see a whole language and understanding unique to you. Assumptions will be made because that's what families do! If you can be clear and explicit about what your family can expect from you and your child, and what you'd like to get from them, it will make everything easier. Tell them what to expect: maybe your child can't cope with large groups of people, so maybe they won't be seeing your child at family gatherings for a while. Perhaps the incessant questions from a certain family member, delivered with a serving of 'not in my day', are creating an ongoing stress. Be clear and explicit about what you do and don't want to happen. Remind them your child is struggling and you could all do with their support. It will save you many nights grumbling about them.

Be open, be honest

I know how hard it is to face the brutal truth of your child's situation. So, whether your child is showing signs of anxiety or they're in crisis or recovery, call it what it is. Be open about it. Be honest about the impact it is having on you all. And don't be ashamed. This is tough, but it is happening. There is no room or justification for shame or blame. We all need to speak mental illness's name.

Set gentle boundaries

Change is hard for the best of us, so a change of routine or availability will likely be received with some resistance. Know that it's OK to push back against that. If you can't continue with the commitments you had before your child's illness, that's OK. Be clear and kind as you assert the new boundaries that are necessary for you and your child. It's not your job to control how other people respond to these new changes, so it's OK to not manage their emotions about what's going on. See this as an extraordinary time, not a forever indication of your whole relationship.

Don't give yourself a hard time

This situation wasn't created by you and it's unfair for you to take the blame for what is happening. Look beyond any harsh words and there may well be years of festering resentment just waiting for an opportunity to burst forth. Ask yourself if your child's illness and whatever behaviour your family member feels is unacceptable has given them an excuse to address grievances from the past.

Ask close family to educate themselves

Not everyone understands mental illness. Not everyone gets that it isn't like a broken leg that you put in plaster and in six weeks it's repaired. But you can ask them to google it or watch the World Health Organization's video about depression on YouTube (search for 'Black Dog'). Don't take it on yourself to educate them. It's enough that your child is ill; you don't need to justify or excuse it with lengthy explanations.

Ask family to help in ways they understand

Asking your family to help in ways that may not feel big or meaningful to others but make a difference to you can enable your family to still feel a part of things when you're battling for your child. Maybe they could help with a bit of housework or ironing. Or if they make a killer shepherd's pie or apple crumble, ask for a delivery now and then. In most cases, they'll want to help but won't know how. Give them a way in, and thank them for their support. It might not be what you really need, but it is what they can offer.

Remember your family is hurting too

However all-consuming your child's illness is, take a moment to step out of your shoes and into theirs. They've seen changes in you and your child – a child who is still a grandchild, a niece or nephew, a cousin. They are grieving the loss of their expectations for your child and their relationship with them. Not everyone is conscious enough to make sense of difficult situations at the time they happen, and this can lead to hurtful remarks or actions.

Be nice

I think sometimes the most helpful thing to be is nice. The last thing you want is to waste precious time berating yourself for ranting at someone for all the things you're cross about. Remember it's not their fault you're here, any more than it is yours, and if they can't support you how you want, that doesn't stop you from being polite and friendly. If you can't make a family get-together or party, send a card wishing them a lovely time and explain a little of why you can't make it. Book in a phone call to catch up. And if that's not good enough, breathe and step back. It doesn't stop you stepping forward in the future. It keeps that open as a possibility.

Respect your child's privacy

Whether you're a large, tight-knit family or there's only a few of you, allow your child to decide how much everyone knows about the detail of what is going on. This can be a hard balance to strike, because you may want to share with your family. I used to share what I thought my daughter would be happy for me to say in front of her. An imperfect metric, but it made me consider my words before launching into a detailed description of everything she was going through.

If in doubt, cut them out

Not necessarily for your whole life, but just for this time. Explain you have a lot on your mind and need to concentrate on getting your child and your immediate family through. Most people will understand, and that honesty and transparency could even open up the conversation and improve the connection.

Navigating These Changing Times

It can be an unnecessary preoccupation to try to unpick why we can't deliver what our relationships demand, and equally why we feel short-changed by them too. Being kind to ourselves when we recognise these shifts, giving ourselves and others space without judgement, not always being up close and personal, and remembering what is the most important thing – our well-being and our child's well-being – can help relieve some of the extraneous stress.

Ultimately, the relationships you have should support you, particularly through this extraordinary time, and you should not be afraid of letting go of those that don't. The efforts to deal with the fight in front of you demand focus and you need nurture, not nastiness, to get through. It's not forever, although you may find you're just too different to pick up where you left off. But when you come through, you will be surrounded by people who love you, who see you and who get you.

Keep in mind . . .

1. Your focus at this time will need to be on your child and you and your immediate family. It can be draining to navigate your friendships and family relationships, and you don't have to be all things to all people.

2. Be clear about what you need and want, whether that is to just have a laugh with a friend, or your mum's home-cooked lasagne, or to be left alone for a week or two.

3. It's not forever – relationships will change, and can improve if you keep communicating.

4. There is a fantastic online community who have been where you are. You are not alone at this time.

12

Handling the Everyday

As you partner your child through daily life you will come across practical challenges, such as diet, sleep, exercise, social media and medication. We'll look in this chapter at how you can partner your child with these 'everyday' issues.

Whether you're reading this because you've just seen the extent of your child's mental health crisis or you've been in the thick of it for some time, reflecting on the things you can change, and making a plan, can bring some order to your own mind and help to support your child too. Accepting the new normal and 'standing beside' (see page 84) your child means working with your child to co-create a new set of rules that build resilient recovery.

The realisation that your child is mentally ill and is not living the life you expected them to is a difficult one to take on board. But I found the 'new normal' easier to come to terms with once I'd made a plan. The new rules needed new approaches and, for me, I needed to write a plan to help me understand the shape of Issy's illness and what I could practically do to support her. You might want to write something down, alongside your partner, or simply have a discussion about the key practical issues. You might just pick out one or two ideas from this chapter. Do whatever works best for you at this time.

This chapter covers some of the things that may be helpful to consider – things that you can have some influence over and aim to optimise to slow the descent (see page 68) of your child's mental health and help support their recovery. It's also worth considering the things you can influence at home and the things that may need to be managed outside of home, like school and work. If you can, I encourage you to confront these head-on and make adjustments; this will help to take the pressure off you and your child. Everything is possible when you make a plan, whether it is to work from home, get schoolwork emailed or push for that emergency appointment. Let's work through some of the things you might need to consider now.

> If, at any time, you think that you cannot keep your child safe, please take them to A&E. Your concerns are real and valid and your worry is not misplaced.

Reading through this, you may feel that some of it is counter-intuitive. Partnering can often feel contrary in the initial stages while you're challenging what you've been told is the right way to behave (see page 82) and while you're building trust in yourself, and with your child.

The adjustments in this chapter have been tried and tested by me and many others in the Parenting Mental Health community to support a child with a mental health condition, but it's a personal recipe for you to test and tweak to find your family's way forward.

> 'We have known for many years that humans heal and flourish in a compassionate environment when we are brave enough to provide it. "When a flower doesn't bloom you don't blame or punish the flower, you change the environment they are in." It can feel frightening to move away from behaviours that feel familiar to you, such as telling your child what to do, how to do it, what they should

think. However, to feel heard, understood, respected and valued are all essential ingredients for an environment that children and indeed adults can thrive in. Being punished and controlled creates shame, guilt and erodes self-esteem, and yet we still can't seem to give up our desire to be in control and to impose our will on others, even when we can see that style of parenting does not create the results and relationship we had hoped for.'

Zanneta Neale, chartered psychologist

Your Home Environment

Have you ever had a friend whose house felt like a calm haven in the chaos of your life? Or did you find that their house *was* the chaos? Could you not wait to escape it and go home to your own space?

In the midst of open-ended uncertainty, the environment we live in – from the look and feel to the atmosphere and even the smell – is something we have control over. We all need somewhere safe to escape to, and that space, safe, warm, under control, is so important in establishing a foundation for recovery for our children. Whether that's their own bedroom or, if they share, a corner of a room (think of Harry Potter, with the cupboard under the stairs), having a space where your child can control the look, feel and flow gives them somewhere to return to when things are tough or they've over-peopled or overstretched themselves.

Your child's room is their haven, but, when they're battling mental illness, it can also be their prison. One moment it's home, the next it's hell, so as well as making their space their haven, finding other environments that can feel like home is important too. The car has long been a favourite space for my children; a place where we can explore the kinds of conversations that aren't easy to have face to face.

My husband and daughter found a cafe that they liked. Quiet and off the beaten track, it was another safe space for her to just be, without fear of judgement or of bumping into people from her old school. She knew what to expect and what would happen, and it got her out of the house (and allowed me some time to clean up her room).

Next, look at the state of the environment. This is not about giving yourself a hard time for a lack of show-home standards, but looking objectively at the space you all live in, through your child's eyes. While most teenagers don't see the dust or the mess, when they're mentally ill, a sense of disorder can impact on their mood, while a sense of order can offer stability and comfort.

Let's start with their personal space. Whatever shape this takes, it's likely that it will not be kept to the kind of standards you expect. Learning to live with the mess and not nag them to clean it up is a skill. The contents of my crockery cupboard were often to be found in my daughter's bedroom. My mission when I went in was to remove as much as I could carry, with the least amount of fuss. Many of her actions were about asserting some level of control over her environment, so I had to show that I respected this with my actions, words and non-verbal communication (see page 135). Saying all this, I didn't give up on making her space calm and comforting. I'd *ask* when it was convenient for me to change her bed. Sometimes even that request was an obligation on her, a reminder that she couldn't do it or hadn't done it, and so I learned to turbo-charge my actions and could change her bedding at lightning speed. I had everything ready, I'd go in and, within two minutes, the bed was changed. Within three minutes, the plates were removed, and by popping on a diffuser or lighting a scented candle, the whole space suddenly felt calmer. At other times I suggested that we try to clean it up together as it would make it more comfortable and comforting for her. As she would move things around, I'd flick a duster or run the hoover over the carpet, without judgement.

Here are some of the things you can try to improve the atmosphere of home and make it a comfort to your child:

- **Remove any visual triggers.** My daughter was out of school for two years and it took a while for us to understand what we were dealing with. We had no idea what the next day would bring, let along the next week, month or term. Was it the right thing or the wrong thing to leave her school bag in the hallway? Would she need her blazer again soon? How about the school calendar? Within about a fortnight of her initial appointment with the psychiatrist, I decided that these reminders could be put away. Placing them in a cupboard didn't mean she wouldn't ever go back, but having them on show wasn't making her any more capable of attending. Take a look at any trigger items that are around your house and put them away. Maybe it's their work uniform, a bag they use for a paper round, the riding hat or the Scout scarf. It's not that you're being actively supportive of them not doing things, it's that you're actively supporting them with the space and understanding they need right now. The aim is always that, at some point in the future, they'll be able to do the things they currently can't.
- **Lighting.** I asked my daughter what made her room most comfortable and she immediately mentioned lighting. Having flexible lighting gave her control over the mood of the space. It gave her the option to sleep with the light on (no, it's not advised for optimum rest, but it was the only way she could nod off) and the peace to erase the darkness in the corners, that may have kept

her awake if she had lain there wondering what might be in those recesses.

- **A Himalayan salt lamp.** Apparently good for anxiety, and such a calming light and an unusual object.
- **An essential oil diffuser.** We used a number of calming essential oil mixes and this definitely helped to improve the sense of calm in the room.
- **Clean bedding.** There's nothing better than clean sheets, is there? And your child probably won't admit it because they might not consciously acknowledge it, but clean bedding can make a world of difference. It's worth asking if they have a favourite bed set, because the sensory benefits they get from being coddled in bed linen they are comforted by is really important when the whole world doesn't make any sense. If this is the case, try to buy another duplicate set. Or install your child on the sofa for the day while you wash and return it.
- **Weighted blankets.** Weighted blankets are known to reduce anxiety and promote good sleep. They can be used on a bed, on the sofa or for car journeys. The weighted blanket gets its weight from the small pellets or beads it is filled with. Blankets come in a variety of weights, which apply pressure to the body – like a hug in blanket form. The pressure is meant to reduce the stress hormone cortisol and apparently encourages the production of serotonin. The sense of comfort and calm they offer many is definitely worth a try. You can make them yourself, but they are readily available online (see page 295).

Changing the atmosphere of family life

There are subtle ways you can change the atmosphere of your home too, other than things like lighting, which can have very positive effects:

- **Toning down the routine.** If your child is functioning enough to access education, consider toning down your interactions around this so they have some space to cope. This could be as simple as not asking how their day went, or speaking to school about a homework break. There's more in the section on how to deal with school (see page 270) and lots of resources on the Parenting Mental Health website (see page 295).
- **Give your child some mental space.** Offer them opportunities to engage but don't demand. Give your child emotional space – don't overload them with your emotions or needs as you go about your day. Meet them where they are.

What not to do

Over in the Parenting Mental Health community on Facebook, I've seen a lot of parents talk about taking the door off their child's room. Personally, I've never done this or considered doing it. I see it as untrusting, disrespectful and, in many cases, a way of fighting fire with fire that only serves to increase the chasm between you and your child. I asked psychologist Zanneta Neale how to deal with this situation:

'Where you feel the need to control, for example, by removing their door or threatening to, try to consider how this would make you feel if someone treated you this way. How are you feeling? What is the outcome you are looking for? How can you include your child in finding a way forward with this particular issue?'

If you feel you must pursue this action, sit yourself down and be honest. Is it a reaction to the situation? A final demonstration that you're in charge? The only thing this demonstrates, in my mind, is that you do not understand your child. It ostracises you from them and, whatever it is that you are trying to achieve, it breaks down the bonds of trust, understanding and tolerance.

Maybe you're thinking of it because you can't trust your child to not harm themselves. The compulsion to self-harm will not subside because the door isn't on. Your child will find alternative places and ways to try to ease their pain, and again feel that they are being ostracised at a time when they need more compassion, more connection and more care.

Partnering is about standing beside our child and travelling together (see page 87), and sometimes we have to respect some of the behaviours we find distasteful or destructive while they work through them. Sometimes we have to recognise that our children aren't a problem to be fixed, they're a flower to allow to blossom.

Living arrangements

If you decide that a more permanent solution is necessary, acting on that need is absolutely OK too. Maybe your child feels that they need to move out. Being under the same roof is not a pre-requisite for a relationship. Maybe you can't agree on the things that are sacred to your family. Or maybe your child needs intensive support that you aren't qualified or able to deliver. Whether your child is in an inpatient facility or you've all decided it is for the best that they live elsewhere for a while, please don't think that that's the end of your relationship or that your relationship is anything less than what it might be if they were living at home. The distance in space and perception that not living at home offers can, in many cases, improve the quality of the relationship over time.

Food and Mealtimes

At the point of depression or anxiety, appetite is one of the first things to change. Our children may want to eat more sugar to escape the lack of feeling, or food may feel like an insult and something to be avoided at all costs. Their sense of taste may also change – maybe they no longer like certain things – and this can mean they are turned off from the act of eating. In some cases, medication can impact on their perception of taste and texture. Mental health issues can also impact on your child's digestion, leading to constipation, diarrhoea and IBS.

Food can also be used as a control mechanism or a reward. Just like us when we're overly stressed, your teenager may turn towards food or turn away from it. I don't know about you, but when someone tells me not to do something, I do it even more, so voicing our issues around food and the amount they are or are not consuming can be the start of a tug of war over something that should be so simple. We have to tread carefully so that we don't turn a simple, short-term response into a psychologically fragile situation.

If you feel your teenager's lack of appetite or overeating is about control rather than physiological due to changes in their taste buds, I urge you to get professional help for them (see page 298).

> **Please note**
>
> If your child is not eating as they usually would, whether due to lack of appetite or changing eating patterns, seek guidance from a doctor. This book does not go into detail about eating disorders. Please seek professional support if you suspect your child has an eating disorder.

The health benefits of food

I learned a lot about food during this time, not least through my own experiments with a gut-friendly diet and the insights I gained from Jane Hutton, a holistic functional nutritionist (see page 301). According to Jane, the function of the brain and its neurotransmitters (chemicals that control our mood, motivation, calm and concentration) is entirely dependent on nutrients, and the best source of these is everyday food. Supplements are a necessary substitute sometimes, but should be professionally advised – getting it wrong, especially if there is medication involved, can result in anything from a waste of money to actively endangering health.

Our bodies and brains are complex, but nourishing ourselves can be very simple. Eat as well, and as fresh and natural, as you can, or call in a professional nutritionist for advice and support if you need to.

At home, there are a few things to aim for:

- Eat regularly, around three meals a day plus small snacks.
- Get enough protein and healthy fats like omega-3 (great 'brain' food) from oily fish.
- Avoid refined carbs, such as white bread, pasta and biscuits.
- Reduce sugar, so avoid fizzy drinks and sweets.
- Eat plenty of fruit and veg, including in smoothies and pasta sauces.

It can be hard for us to get nutrient-rich foods into our children, but knowing the importance of it can help us to make small shifts to try to improve the quality of what they eat.

Keeping the gut healthy

Gut health is crucial – the gut is where our food is digested and nutrients released, with gut bacteria increasingly indicated in supporting mental health. Nutritionists like Jane who specialise in mental health nutrition can now work with supplementing specific strains of gut bacteria that research has proven to help conditions like anxiety. Most importantly, when it is filled with good bacteria, our gut is capable of changing the way our body and brain work. The right probiotic supplement can work wonders (while using the wrong probiotic or fermented food can end up achieving very little except a lighter wallet or unpleasant symptoms!). It's worth noting that stress and anxiety can cause gut inflammation via the gut–brain connection, so there can be a vicious circle set up where children need the nutrients to balance mood, but anxiety itself has inflamed the gut, causing tummy aches and inefficient digestion, so nutrients are not sufficiently ingested or well absorbed.

When we eat a nutrient-poor diet, our gut can fill with nasty bacteria, which are responsible for a demise in our mental and physical health.

How to make eating well less stressful

So, how can you deal with the issue of food and quality food without nagging your child or making them feel under pressure? Here are some ideas for you to consider:

- **Chill out a bit.** No, it's not ideal to live off junk food and it won't be supporting good gut health, but it is possible in the short term. If your child is eating something, even if it's not healthy by your terms, they are getting calories in.
- **Make it easy for them.** Getting nutrients into our bodies is important for mental health and doing it through a wide range of natural food, rather than supplements, is best. Making milkshakes or smoothies with fresh fruit, adding extra vegetables to chilli or pasta sauces, or even using beetroot, squash or black beans in baking can add some much-needed nutrients. Leave healthier dishes of snacks or nibbles around to see if they'll pick from them. According to Jane, deficiencies in certain nutrients can actually reduce appetite and affect taste buds – this is where some key foods, even as ordinary as bananas and live yoghurt, can be game changers, as they are packed with nutrition and easy to eat. Adding little gem lettuce

or spinach gives some green goodness without tasting too much of vegetables.

- **Get your child involved.** Encourage your child to prep their own food or to help you. A child is more likely to have appetite for a food they have chosen. Try to involve your child in the planning of meals – even if it's just one meal a week – as a way to understand what they might be more open to trying or what they really don't like.

- **Provide plenty of drinks.** There are lots of possibilities when it comes to making hydration exciting, such as having a jug of water in the fridge with fruit slices macerating in it, to create flavoured water. Smoothies, milkshakes and soups are easy ways to combine eating and drinking. Reducing fizzy drinks and squashes stuffed with chemicals can be a challenge – their flavour can make them a first choice – but their effect on blood sugar levels means they actively contribute to anxiety and mood swings. Herbal teas can be popular, but coffee can contribute to mood swings and interfere with sleep (see page 229).

- **Monitor but don't manage.** It's time to take a deep breath and go with the flow. The more of an issue your child's food intake is to you, the more of an issue it is likely to become for them. You might like to note down what they ate today; you may be reassured at what they are actually taking in. It's worth quietly checking their bins for wrappers – you might find they don't want to eat with the family but are taking calories in from snacks.

- **Give your child some space.** Maybe they're anxious about eating in front of others; maybe they eat slower than everyone else and feel the spotlight is on them because of this. While family meals are a great time to connect, if food is becoming an issue, let it go for a while and see how they respond. Ask your child if they'd like a tray to eat somewhere else. Your child really doesn't want to feel that they're being managed or that there is extra pressure on them. You have the power to not make this into a battle.

- **Give your child the facts.** If knowledge is power, our children may need to hear some facts about the requirements of the human body. Jane Hutton says we run on nutrients, not just calories, and our bodies need 90 different nutrients a day to function at optimum levels. It's unlikely your child is getting close to this (like many adults!), but it could be the impetus they need to take control of their diet and even 'gamify' their food intake. Reflect on what interests or connects with your child and see how this kind of information could help them. One idea is to draw up a list of 30 plant foods, such as beans, pulses, veg, fruit, grains and so on – that slice of toast, tub of hummus, dollop of jam and carrot stick can all count. Your teen can tick them off and see how they are doing on the variety front.

- **Think about how to get nutrients in.** If you are worried about your child not eating enough, or your doctor has advised, there are easy ways to supplement a diet, and it might take some of the worry out for you. There are unflavoured liquid vitamin and mineral formulas that can be added to drinks so that your child won't know they're taking them, if that's an issue.

- **See the best in the food you give them.** If your child's diet is limited, think about what they will eat and see how you can upgrade the nutrients by buying less processed produce or adding extra nutrients in. For example, Jane recommends baked beans on buttered toast as a go-to food for your child, as it is packed with protein. You could add some fresh spinach leaves under the beans and some cheese grated on top too. Add some green beans to a curry, serve some corn on the cob with a burger or finish a meal with a bowl of fresh fruit. By seeing the best, and not concentrating on what is missing, we can take the pressure off us all.

- **Try to set a positive example.** How are you about food? Is it a big deal? Do you eat regularly? Please don't see this as an opportunity to kick yourself, but do consider how your behaviour could be seen by your child. If it's an issue to you, use this as an opportunity to try to heal that part in you, and find support if you need it.

The Power of Sleep

As the Irish proverb goes: 'A good laugh and a long sleep are the two best cures for anything.' Changing sleep behaviour is likely to be an indicator to you that something is wrong with your child's mental health, and it may become yet another battleground if you expect it to be as it was before they got ill.

My daughter's psychiatrist made it clear to us that good sleep was a priority for strong mental health, and we agreed, but saying that good sleep is essential and moving towards that can feel like an impossible task when your child has depression or anxiety. Many nights I heard my daughter padding around upstairs at stupid o'clock. Consumed by her thoughts and fears, she found it hard to rest, generally falling asleep as I was getting up. And the cycle continued. She isn't alone. So many young people and families are dealing with shifted sleep patterns. It can be hugely frustrating to watch it and not feel able to make any changes.

A lack of sleep can mask what is really going on in our child's mental health. Overtiredness or disordered sleep can lead to frustration, anger and aggression, particularly when we expect a child to work on a 'normal' timetable when they've only had a handful of hours' sleep.

So, how can you navigate a lack of sleep or when your child is living at the wrong end of the day? The first thing that doesn't help is telling your child they have to change! It might sound obvious, but, right now, they don't have the same expectations of time or 'rules' and are unlikely to be in a place to be able to 'just go to bed earlier'. They have a routine; it's just not the one on your timetable.

Speak to them about their sleep without judgement. Ask: What is keeping you up? Is it anxiety? Is it that their only friend lives on the other side of the world and speaking to them makes them feel less isolated?

Depending on where they are on the curve (see page 67), if they are ready to begin to own their recovery, you can have a gentle chat about the impact of sleep. Use a range of other people's experiences as vehicles to share the kind of information that you want your child to understand. Facts about sleep aren't exciting until you're middle-aged, so talk about the impact and outcome of less sleep. No judgement. Just give them the info and see if it seeps in. For example, say that scientists have found that getting enough sleep each day can really boost mood; that drinking coffee might make you feel awake, but it might stop you sleeping later; or that researchers at Stanford University have found that teenagers' circadian rhythm shifts to a later time, making it biologically harder to fall asleep after 11pm.

If they are open to discussing changing their behaviour to improve their mental health, you could discuss getting a regular routine in place. For example, lights out at 11pm. It might be 2am for your teen, but that's a start – it's a routine.

Phones and sleep disruption

One of the hardest things for our teenagers is stepping away from the mobile phone. The blue light emitting from devices slows our body's ability to make melatonin, the hormone that regulates our sleep patterns. As a result, phone use late at night can prevent us falling asleep easily. We didn't restrict phone usage for Issy – it was her lifeline – but if you feel you want to, I suggest having an open conversation about it. If your child is in crisis, they might be using it to chat with one of the text services or connect with friends who can help them with their thoughts, which seem to be more intrusive and potentially dangerous at night. If you want to try to remove phones from bedrooms, discuss it as a family and lead by example. We parents can be as glued to our devices as our children, yet don't seem to hold ourselves up to the same scrutiny.

Caffeine and other stimulants

Too much caffeine can keep our brains and bodies too wired to rest. Caffeine should ideally be avoided, but, if not, reduced around four hours before your child heads to bed. Limit the amount of products with caffeine in the house. And it's not just coffee and tea – colas and energy drinks have caffeine in them, with even greater amounts in some of the diet options.

An overload of emotions

Many of my best conversations with Issy happened when she couldn't sleep. Talking it out helped her to come to a resolution, and then to rest. But if there is an overload of emotion, our brains can carry on trying to work out a solution into the small hours. Sometimes we can't change that for our children, but we can understand its impact on their ability to sleep. Helping them with their sleep hygiene and other suggestions in this section may help to alleviate this, but sometimes you will just have to accept where you are today.

Making a bedroom sleep-friendly

Creating the right environment for sleep is so important. Look at your child's room and see if you can make it sleep-ready with some of the ideas below. Introducing some of these can create a sense of routine, such as making a warm drink before you all go to bed or turning on the music or night light, which can help to introduce sleep patterns.

- **Low lighting.** A night light can give a familiar security.
- **Reduce stress.** Remove rubbish and clutter from their room to help keep it calm.
- **Reduce light coming in.** It might be time to consider blackout curtains to ensure that they can maximise the number of hours they sleep.
- **Comforting noise.** Repetitive, low-level sounds are non-threatening and allow the brain to relax into a calmer state. Listening to ASMR (autonomous sensory meridian response), such as a rain soundtrack, can be very soothing, or they may prefer a meditation app like Calm or listening to classical music.
- **Keep the temperature of the room cool.** If it's too hot or too cold, your child will struggle to sleep.
- **Comfy, clean bedding and pillows.** Make sure they have warm, comfy bedding and pillows, suitable for the time of year. Clean sheets are always lovely too (see page 220).

- **Relaxing scents.** Use natural room scents like lavender, valerian and bergamot that encourage sleep. You can use a natural oil diffuser, a sleep spray for their pillow or a roll-on for their forehead.
- **Hot water bottle.** Offer a hot water bottle – they can be really comforting.
- **Bedtime drinks.** Suggest a hot drink like a 'sleepy' herbal tea or a glass of warm milk.

Medical ways to help with sleep

Your child's psychiatrist or GP may suggest an aid to help your child get more sleep. Melatonin is regularly prescribed for sleep, as a natural supplement. It works for lots of people, and may help your child get to sleep when they are struggling to doze off. We found that its efficacy waned over time, so it's important to try to make other adjustments, as above, to support a more positive sleep schedule.

An antihistamine is often also prescribed; promethazine, for example, is used for short-term sleep issues as it makes you drowsier than other antihistamines. As with all medications, you should consult a doctor or pharmacist before giving to your child.

Getting outside during the day

If you can get your child to leave the house, another natural and free sleep support is exercise. A walk and some fresh air, every day, is helpful in regulating the body. Most of our young people are vitamin D-deficient and a walk a day can help increase their levels (depending on the time of year and where you live). There are a lot of studies about the positive mental

health benefits of being among green nature too, so walking in woods among trees can also help. Exercise will also physically tire your teen (see page 235) and help them to drop off, even if their mind has other ideas.

Progress not perfection

Remember, your child has an illness and they are also in their adolescence, which is a time of changing sleep patterns. Your teen may have disrupted sleep for some time. This is not about perfection, it's about progress, trying to help them get more sleep and improve patterns. If that means a nap on the sofa in the afternoon, that's OK. If your child is in crisis, look at it as you did when you had a newborn – sleep when they do. You need to ensure you're not sleep-deprived too. It won't be like this forever, but take the sleep when you can. Think of quality,

rather than quantity. Let go of the judgement on the hours they keep for now; it does change over time.

Exercise and Activities

Exercise and activities that your child has done in the past can be a hindrance or a help, and it's for you to determine which they are to your child. While exercise is proven to improve mood, if it's a team sport that makes your child anxious, the upside will be written off. If they are happy to swim or go to the gym, fantastic. But maybe you'll need to encourage exercise in more unusual ways at this time, and going forward:

- Ask your child to walk the dog with you, or see if you can borrow your neighbour's dog.
- Go for a walk around the block. If your teen doesn't want to go out, this is a good option as it's finite and not too far; it's hard to say no to that.
- Get them to help you clear out the garage or kitchen cupboards, which involves moving around and lifting and sorting.
- Ask for help with the gardening.

Think about the act of using energy, rather than structured sports – these absolutely have a place, but if your child is in crisis, they possibly won't be able to engage right now, and that can make them feel worse.

Activities and hobbies that engage your child and give them something else to focus on are important at this time – to bring them pleasure, and to raise their self-esteem and feelings that they are capable of something.

Encourage your teen to continue with things that they enjoy; this may include gaming or watching TV, but put other opportunities their way too. Consider crafts – making things, painting, colouring, knitting, building Lego, baking . . . things that help them get into 'flow', that state of being completely immersed in the moment. Think about reading or watching TV together so you can discuss the book or programme.

Mindless tasks that have a start and an end are good too – rearranging the cutlery drawer, sorting the washing, tidying a cupboard. They sound simple, and probably a little dull, but each of these things gave my daughter something to do and a sense that she was still capable and was helpful, even if mental illness meant she couldn't leave the house or go to school. We didn't make tasks a fixed routine; it was based on her openness to it on the day. This is not an opportunity to demand your teen complete chores; that will only add to your stress, and theirs.

Personal Hygiene

It's likely you'll face the challenges of your child not wanting to wash at some point. Not just today or tomorrow, but possibly for weeks or months at a time. It's a normal by-product of mental health issues and can come from a lack of motivation or desire to take care of themselves. Your child may feel they don't deserve to be clean, or that there's no point because they won't be able to leave the house anyway, or, worse, they won't be around long enough, so what's the point. They may have sensory or body image issues because of their mental state and it may just be too much. They may see it as something we're forcing upon them to break a bad mental state and they may not want that. It's possibly not logical to you, but it makes perfect sense to them.

If you want to remain engaged, you might have to lower your own standards and change the way you feel about it, to not create a chasm between the two of you. It's not an assault on you, although it might feel like it at times. It's also not a reflection of your parenting or your child's view of you. It is a wholly personal experience, likely a need to feel in control and safe. Exposing your body to water isn't always as relaxing as we might see it.

Let it go. It's OK. Don't go on about it. Be led by them. They will decide when the time is right for them to make progress and you asking if they've had a shower really won't help. Small acts of hygiene are brilliant steps forward. Brushing hair or teeth (or both) or washing hands is a step towards larger, more challenging things, like a shower.

The Online World

Gaming, social media, chat rooms and other online activities, like shopping and reading, can be a real sore point for many parents, and it certainly gets discussed a lot in our online community. Our children are growing up in a world where these actions are normal and expected. Having open conversations about online safety and what feels good and what doesn't can help ensure that, if there is an issue, your child can talk to you about it. Again, it's about suspending judgement and understanding *why* they're doing it. Online communities tend to reflect the groups of people we find in real life. It's for us to find our kind of people, because they give us a sense of belonging and support, so although you need to be aware of potential issues, sometimes we parents need to notice the good things too.

Gaming

Gaming is an important part of a lot of young people's lives and the communities that build up around it can be a support network for them. It's not all good, of course, but then again, neither is life.

You might see gaming as the devil and something that is not helping your child. But gaming is likely to be an activity that can bring them joy at a time when they can't see anything but darkness. You can fight it and them, or you can find a way to understand it and ensure they're using it as safely and positively as possible. Gaming was important for Issy because it gave her a safe, yet challenging space to escape to. It enabled her to find other like-minded people and connect with them when that wasn't possible in the 'real world'. It became a positive anchor in her life, and was a gateway to a number of other associated and positive activities (see page 275).

Firstly, let's look at what gaming might give your child:

- Fun! It gives them fun when they might find it hard to engage with people or even feel the sensation of pleasure.
- Gaming suspends their reality in a crisis and they can escape to a world they have more control over.
- Gaming offers community and support from people who may be going through similar situations.
- Your child can act without impunity. This is not always good, but they may be able to express emotions that they don't feel they can share in person, and this can be a valuable outlet.

- They get a sense of achievement as they improve, win or go up a level. They may not be winning at life in their eyes, but gaming gives them something they can win at.

Ask your child (without judgement) what they like about gaming. What does it give them?

It's so important to challenge your views and, to do that, you need to understand what gaming is. They may be gaming on a PC, a console or a tablet or phone, playing games either alone, in teams or against people around the world. See page 295 for video information on the Parenting Mental Health website that describes what gaming is and why your child might enjoy it so much when they're mentally ill.

Social media

Social media, like all technologies, can be a force for amazing good as well as bad. It has the power to impact on self-esteem and self-worth, in positive and negative ways. It can be seen as the enemy, when it's simply the facilitator and magnifier of human behaviour and emotion.

Your child is using it, possibly as you do, as a way to connect with people, pure and simple. They may be using it as part of a community of people with similar interests. Fandoms, Facebook groups, Discord, anything with a community element, while not immune to nastiness, tend to be positive spaces where people want to come together around a shared passion. They may be using it to chat to people they know in person and connect with people they don't know, and they may find their own peer-group community to understand their emotions and explore their illness. Your teen may be using it to test boundaries and explore social situations, needs and fascinations from the comfort of their bedroom.

Social media platforms also offer an opportunity for creativity and self-expression. Depending on the approach your child has, they offer the potential for a positive feedback loop, whether they're sharing videos, blogs or photos. Of course, this has the potential to tip over into negative behaviours, which is why open, honest conversations are so important around technology use. This isn't always easy, when we can see the dangers and so desperately want to protect our child.

For your child, there is no difference between online and offline; they exist in a universe that's always on. As parents of a certain age, we have a responsibility to understand the platforms and their unique nuances if we are going to be able to have measured, responsible conversations and make informed, reasoned decisions. It's not all cyber-bullying and nudes shared, just like it's not all cat videos and kindness. It is humanity's needs, desires and dark sides played out for free and for all to see, and that is liberating and scary in equal measure, particularly when your child is fighting mental illness.

As humans, we have a rich history of condemning that which we don't know. From the romantic novel of the nineteenth century, to the telephone and TV in the fifties and sixties, it's far too easy for us to make judgement on the new and focus on the risks, rather than consider the potential rewards as well.

According to psychologist Zanneta Neale, most teenagers have a heightened concern about how they are viewed by others and, during this time of trying to forge their own identity and independence, social media is a perfect place to get instant reactions from others and also to have access to others' ideas and thoughts. Teenagers often seek new and exciting experiences due to the continued development of the emotional regions of the brain, and social media is a quick and easy way for them to test and explore those.

TALKING ABOUT SOCIAL MEDIA

You may dislike social media because of what you perceive it to be, or perceive your child to be exposed to, rather than what you know. Finding out, without judgement, how your child uses social media is a starting point. What do they like about it? What don't they like about it? Where is the value to them? What do they do if they feel overwhelmed? (See page 295 for resources about social media sites.)

All behaviour is communication, so if your child is using social media as a way to engage in risk-taking activities, it's not only the activity you need to address, it's the underlying reasons for that behaviour. Speaking about upholding positive personal values around respect, language, our power and our differences is important.

Discuss the concept of your child's 'power'. By this I mean the sense of security and self that comes from living by their own values. Discuss the idea of the 'sense of peace' that comes with knowing that you're in control of what you share about yourself, and what people see and know about you. Sharing a nude photo may make a teen feel flattered and wanted, but there's a 'transfer of power' sent along with the bits and bytes over the ether. When the person who receives it shares it to make themselves feel better and more popular, that simple share gives away the sender's power.

Can't we just ban screen time?

If you are managing your child's social media or online usage, why is that? Do you believe you can control their mental illness by controlling their access? There are no right and wrong answers, and every family and situation is unique, but you may be misunderstanding why your child is reliant on their tech. I know many families where technology enables the only human connection for their child. It also powers curiosity when a child is not able to access education. What are you teaching them if you shut down their choices or don't engage in conversations or behaviours to help them understand their values and boundaries? I don't know the answers to these questions because they will depend on your circumstances, but I feel they're important questions to ask.

Start by having open conversations about it and hold your judgement back that it's all a waste of time. This won't engender any trust and will show you don't understand. Trust them based on their behaviour and be interested and involved. Not by befriending them or following them on every platform (unless they're OK with that), but by making it something they can share with you, without fear of judgement or punishment.

'Fitting in' – the need for our children to follow behaviours and beliefs of their friends – is really strong. Blaming the tech for these very human responses can isolate our children further.

Monitor your teen's tech usage and the impact it has, by all means, and create a space where you can have open conversations without fear of lies or overreactions. If use of tech is causing more sleep issues, then have that conversation, but the aim needs to be to understand *why* your teen is using tech and work out *together* how to fit that in while working towards better mental health.

Medication, Therapies and Supplements

Sitting in the psychiatrist's room and taking the prescription for antidepressants she had just written for my 14-year-old daughter was not a high point of my parenting 'career'. But, it was the start of Issy's recovery. We were too close to suicide for me not to agree with it.

If you're faced with an option of medication, it's not an admission of failure, or a sign that you're a bad parent, or that your child will be on medication for the rest of their life. Medication can be the stabiliser that your child needs to get them to a place of potential for recovery. We believe it was a literal lifesaver for our daughter. If she had needed medication for another condition, I would not have questioned it, so why the issue with antidepressants?

We have to break down the belief that mental illness is something we can love away. We can't. We need to change the environment, change the expectations and sometimes we also need to medicate. Sometimes it's because we can't make enough change in environment and expectation quickly enough. Sometimes we can. Sometimes we don't need meds. But sometimes we do.

Not all medications work the same for everyone. There are lots of studies on the efficacy of antidepressants and some of us are simply immune to them. Remember that mental illness is born from biological, social and psychological inputs, so medication won't always help.

If it is available to you (generally in North America, but not so widespread in the UK, Europe, Australia and New Zealand), get a tolerance test. This is a blood or saliva test that checks the DNA make-up of your child, how they will metabolise certain medications and the likelihood of side effects from a number of popular antidepressants. It's in its infancy as a method and so, while it's worth doing if you can, it's not an option for all.

Medication takes around six to eight weeks to work, and you may see a dip in your child's mental health before you see an improvement, so it's worth keeping an even closer eye on them in the first few weeks. There are some side effects from medication too, but your GP or psychiatrist should go through these with you in detail. My daughter's psychiatrist said that her treatment would be finite. She would get her well and then look to reduce her medication. And she kept her word. My daughter came off her antidepressants after 18 months. It isn't forever, but it's there for as long as it's needed.

Are there any alternatives?

Before we ended up in that psychiatrist's room, we tried all manner of supplements and alternatives for Issy, from brain-enhancing minerals to Rescue Remedy. I was blinkered to medication because I thought that it meant we were going down a one-way road to a life of antidepressants. I judged that I was a failure to have a child on antidepressants. I soon shifted my approach.

You can try herbal or alternative therapies, but speak to a herbalist or a nutritionist before you do so. Levels of vitamin D and other hormones need a blood test for accurate dosages, so don't just pick something off a shelf in the chemist. Cannabidiol (CBD) oil is growing in popularity for its benefits to sleep, anxiety and mood. The World Health Organization has reviewed the safety and effectiveness of CBD oil and concluded: 'CBD is generally well tolerated with a good safety profile.' But there has been very little research into its use in adolescents and, when the brain is at a crucial point in its development, it's important to exercise caution. As with all supplements, CBD oil can interact with other medications, so taking advice from a professional is recommended.

Talking therapy

There are lots of therapeutic methods that can help your child manage and cope with different elements of their mental health issues and different diagnoses.

Cognitive behavioural therapy (CBT) is a popular talking therapy that aims to help manage problems by changing the way we think. CBT has been used since the sixties, and works on the basis that it is not an event that upsets us, but the meaning we give to it. CBT helps us to acknowledge the 'automatic thoughts' we have and step outside of ourselves to challenge them.

Dialectical behaviour therapy (DBT) is based on CBT but brings together two opposites – acceptance and change – to offer a balance that the person in therapy is accepted as they are, alongside a focus on change. DBT has four 'modules': core mindfulness, distress tolerance, emotion regulation and interpersonal effectiveness, with sessions taken both one-to-one and in groups.

For trauma and post-traumatic stress disorder (PTSD), there are a number of therapies, including eye movement desensitisation and reprocessing (EMDR) and BrainWorking recursive therapy (BWRT), that can help. EMDR works by making side-to-side eye movements, with support from the therapist, while you recall the trauma. BWRT is a therapy where you don't have to share the details to benefit. Based in the latest neuroscience and being trialled by the NHS in the UK, BWRT helps new response patterns to be created. Your GP or psychiatrist will suggest which therapies they think would work best for your child, but this may be limited to those generally available. Research what therapies have worked for others in similar circumstances, and don't be afraid to make suggestions to the professionals. There is more information on these approaches in the Resources section on page 295.

Hypnotherapy is also a powerful and useful therapy and can make a big difference to anxiety conditions. Hypnotherapy uses hypnosis – a trance-like mental state where we are hyper-aware, more open to suggestion and generally calmer – to explore anxieties and phobias. Once the hypnotherapist has taken your child into deep relaxation, they will guide them through their feelings and reactions and suggest ways they can modify their behaviour. Hypnotherapy should not be used with psychosis or certain types of personality disorder.

Counselling is a gentle approach for your child to explore their mental health issues. The sense of being 'heard', and not fixed, can lead to an openness to engage with other therapies.

Art, play and music therapy can all help a child explore their emotions and build rapport with their therapist in a non-threatening, safe way, and help them to express the emotions that they may find it so difficult to express in words. Creative therapies work for all ages, and you need a therapist who has been trained in these approaches. You may be able to access some of these therapies through CAMHS, depending on their services, but you can also find a private therapist through Creative Counsellors' Association (see page 300).

Find what works for your child, and someone who works for them too. Rapport, connection and trust are vitally important if your child is going to benefit from the therapeutic experience. These take time to build up and, if your child is flagging up their discomfort with a therapist, it might be that they are being challenged prematurely by them and don't yet feel safe or understood enough to share. You can provide the safe and constant space at home that can allow them to build the rapport with their therapist, but, if your teen and the therapist aren't suited, know that moving on isn't failure; it's simply part of the journey to find what works for your child. Approaching therapy as an experiment, not a guarantee, can help take the pressure off you both.

Keep in mind . . .

1. Home is a haven during mental health recovery and there are ways you can make it more comfortable for your teen, and for you too.
2. Food, exercise and sleep are key to positive mental health. There are no 'quick fixes' but you can take gentle steps forward in all these areas.
3. Medication can be a positive way out of crisis for some. It's not forever, and there are many options available.
4. Therapy is about finding ways to ease your child's pain, while knowing that this isn't a quick fix. It's about understanding the issues around their mental illness and where it has come from; to uncover the reasons behind the illness, and treat those so your child can become stronger and more resilient. Together, with the professionals, you can begin the important work of helping your child to repair and rebuild.

13

Dealing With the Professionals

Your child's recovery from mental illness is a team effort and your place on that team is essential. So being heard by professionals is vital if you're going to work together to make recovery happen.

Your child is likely to need support from others if they are going to recover from a mental health problem, including from doctors, psychiatrists, therapists and school. It's not always easy to access this support or understand how to make it work for the benefit of your child. This chapter is a guide to dealing with the main points of contact in your child's life outside of the family, both to support them appropriately and to support you as you navigate this unique time.

You'd expect that, at a time of crisis, everyone would be open and ready to support whatever is required to help speed the recovery of your child. However, I've heard from many, many parents who feel they are not heard by the professionals involved in their child's care, and their knowledge and reflections are dismissed as insignificant. Sometimes parents feel overlooked due to their child's age or capability to take charge of their own care. Sometimes it feels like there's an expectation that we parents have done something to make this mental illness appear or hang around. Sometimes it's as if we're just there to chauffeur and cook. Certainly, the challenges that mental health services in the UK face with funding, resources and demand impact on the amount of time and care available. Stripped back to the bone, there isn't the capacity to connect with parents, with the child's health being the rightful priority. It's not always easy, but there are a lot of committed and compassionate mental health professionals out there as well as a lot of useful support. So let's go through the options.

The GP

Usually, your first point of contact if you are concerned about your child's health is with a GP, so let's start there. So many parents join the Parenting Mental Health community when they don't know where to go next. The symptoms of mental illness, such as outbursts, worries, fear and changes in sleeping, eating and moods, seem like the sort of things parents should be able to manage. The more people I speak to, however, the more I think we should reach out for professional help sooner, not later. We wouldn't stick a plaster on a broken leg or a sprained ankle; we'd take the issue to a specialist, explain what has happened and ask them to help.

Going to see your doctor about your child's mental health changes and challenges is not an admission of failure. In fact, it is responsible. It is the best thing you can do. It can say to your child: I hear you, you're important. We all have mental health and, sometimes, like our physical health, it needs some attention.

What if your child doesn't want to see a doctor?

There are lots of reasons why your child may not want to see a doctor. Maybe they see it as a failure in themselves. Maybe they're unsure what it will entail and are scared of what might

happen. Maybe they're scared that people will find out and talk about them. Maybe they can't face the truth of their declining mental state or believe it's for them to 'pull themselves together'. Facing the facts of your own mental health issues is tough. It can feel like you're losing your sense of self and, for a young person who is trying to find their place in the world and understand how it works, 'fessing up' to that is tough.

Talking to your child about their mental health will begin some time before you decide to go and see a doctor. Speaking to them openly about their feelings, challenges and any solutions they think may improve their mental health is enriching for you both and can connect you. Make it clear to your child that there is absolutely no shame in saying you are in need of support. Talk through the idea of seeing a doctor and decide to make an appointment together. If you can, avoid springing a doctor's appointment on your child without warning.

If your child is adamant that they don't want to see a doctor, you can go and see the doctor yourself and share your concerns. I understand how isolating and scary it is to have a child whose mental health means they can't function. I know how painful it is to see their fizz for life dissolve and have no idea how to deal with it. Sometimes going and speaking to your doctor without your child can be helpful to *you*. Asking the doctor if they have any suggestions can sometimes make us feel like we're being useful, and can be a helpful step forward.

If your child absolutely won't go to the doctor, an alternative is to make an appointment for something else. Maybe you've 'seen/heard/made up' that there's an MOT for teenagers, or something similar, available. Speak to your doctor, explain what your plan is and let your child go in on their own, if age-appropriate. They may open up to the doctor, they may hear something from them to make them feel that it's OK to talk about mental health or the doctor might be able to share some information that gives them some under-the-radar options to engage with.

Steps towards recovery

Recovery begins when your child decides they want to get well, so you may find yourself in a little game while they become comfortable with the fact they are in need of professional support. This is OK. It is their illness. It is their experience. We are here to support and walk beside them, not fix them, for as long as it takes.

The first GP appointment

That first appointment to see your doctor about your child is an important step to getting access to effective support and treatment, acknowledging what your child is facing and letting them know that you take it seriously and you care about their mental health. I would urge you to see your doctor as soon as you feel something isn't right. The slow descent, and the fast one into crisis, can be halted by intervention: intervention from professionals *and* changes in your behaviour. Before we discuss the kinds of interventions that you can expect to access through your GP, I'd like you to consider two key things:

1. Be clear and definitive so you can access the right support for your child.
2. Demonstrate to your child that they matter, you have heard them and you are taking their situation seriously.

COMMUNICATING WHAT IS GOING ON

To be clear and definitive, sit with a piece of paper and pen and note down the reason for your visit. When I first took my daughter to see the doctor, I took him a letter I had written explaining why we were there. I didn't think there was any way I would be able to explain everything that was going on or my thoughts on it in the allotted time. I covered some of what had happened, some of my daughter's symptoms and also added in all of the things I thought might have contributed. You can read the letter I wrote on the Parenting Mental Health website (see page 295).

Start by free writing. Pour out all the things you're worried about. An example might start with: 'I just don't know what to do. Jimmy isn't sleeping and won't go to school. I don't know what's going on. It's having an impact on us all. He's stopped eating and everything is a struggle. I can't seem to change anything. I don't know what to do and I'm about to get fined by school.'

I expect, if this is the first time you've seen the GP, you'll have a huge amount of worry, fear and uncertainty to get out on paper. Let rip! Get it all out and not only will you feel better for putting it down on paper, but you'll have probably noted down some useful information. Look back at what you wrote. You now need to edit it and make it information-rich, yet concise. The best way I have found to do this is to answer the following questions, in this order:

- **Who?** *Who* are you going to speak to the GP about? This is to make it clear as you sit down that this is an appointment for your child.
- **What?** *What* is happening that is out of the ordinary? Give a concrete example, rather than a vague notion. The doctor needs to understand what is different about your child. What was normal and what is now not normal? For example, saying he's not sleeping can be vague. Is it that his sleep pattern has shifted? Or is he awake earlier in the morning? Is he struggling to fall asleep? Or stay asleep? Start to look into the detail of what is going on and put yourself in the doctor's shoes. He doesn't know your child. He needs to be shown examples of changes to be able to see the impact on your child and on you as a family.
- **When?** *When* did it start? Or how long have you seen these symptoms? You may not be able to answer when it started, but your child may. What you can offer in this opening gambit to the doctor is an idea of whether this started last week or last year.
- **Why?** *Why* did it start? This may be an educated guess on your part or your child might be able to share some of the reasons why they are in need of support for their mental health. I've seen over the past few years that there may be several reasons why we think a child's mental health deteriorates, but your child is the key to understanding

what the actual trigger is. If you can't answer this question, it's better to skip this one for now than try to come up with your own versions of their reality. It could be alienating for your child and can give the doctor inaccurate information at a time where clarity is important.

Now, once you have all of that information to hand, you can start to write a simple, clear outline of why you want to see the doctor that isn't overly emotional (because that's not fair on your child) but is clear enough for the doctor to understand exactly what is going on.

Let's try an example: 'We're here today to talk about Jimmy. We've noticed that he is finding it hard to get to sleep at night. His sleep schedule has shifted and he is now not able to get to sleep before 5am. He has become too anxious to leave the house and can't go to school. He's been anxious for the past six months but it has escalated in the past three weeks. We don't know why it has got worse, and neither does Jimmy, although he was bullied at school last year.'

This will give the doctor an idea of what is going on and a starting point to ask your child questions.

Giving your child space

When we went to see our doctor, I explained that I knew he had to tell me everything about my daughter as she was underage, but he corrected me. If a child under the age of 16 is deemed to be competent, they can take charge of their care and choose to exclude parents from it, although doctors do have a duty to share when they believe a child is at risk or in danger.

When my daughter asked to see the doctor on her own when we returned for the first interim appointment, it was disconcerting for me, but as parents we have to give them space to talk. Your child may not want you to hear what they feel. If they are suicidal, as my daughter was, telling someone you want to end your life in front of your mum makes a desperate situation even more difficult. My daughter also knew that I would be emotional and, to be honest, she didn't need to deal with that too.

Managing your own emotions

Veiled in the act of caring, we can find ourselves making our feelings about our children the primary focus of interactions with professionals, rather than their feelings and what's really going on. It's natural and normal and nothing to be ashamed of, but something we need to keep in check. Delegating your anxiety isn't fair, and it's so easily done because we're overwrought and spilling over with emotions. There are other ways of letting that out, including seeing professionals for your own support (see page 295).

Wherever you are in the world, your child has a right to privacy. Yes, even about something as life-challenging and -changing as their mental health. Article 16 of the UN Convention on the Rights of the Child states: 'No child shall be subjected to arbitrary or unlawful interference with his or her privacy, family, home or correspondence, nor to unlawful attacks on his or her honour and reputation.'

Please don't assume you will have the right to know everything, and make this a point of conflict with professionals or your child. You might not like it, but it's your child's right.

Your child is more likely to share with you as you pause judgement and partner them through their illness. Take a look at Chapter 8 for ideas on how to create an environment where you can have more open conversations if you feel you need to know more about what is going on.

What if you feel your doctor isn't 'listening'?

So often we feel we don't have a voice, particularly when it comes to dealing with learned professionals who have seen hundreds or thousands of parents like us. We were fortunate to have excellent care from the doctors who have supported our family through mental illness, but I know not every parent has the same experience.

In light of this, consider how you see your interactions with professionals. They've trained long and hard to get to the position they are at, and have seen countless cases just like your child's over the time they have practised. They've seen the curve (see page 67) in practice many times. They have an approach that they believe to work generally. They are there to do what they believe to be the best for your child, based on the information they have been given and within the constraints of their working practices. They deserve to be dealt with in a respectful manner and spoken to politely. It is not their fault that waiting lists are long or that certain treatments aren't available to your child due to budget issues, so my tip is to try to keep some of those (valid) frustrations to yourself. Try to see the wider context that they are working in.

> I believe our job as parents is to respect the professionals' experience and knowledge and to listen to them. And then to challenge it, politely, if we don't believe it to be the most appropriate course of action for our child.

As an advocate for our children, it is so important to speak up. With respect to the professionals, our child is one of a number of patients. The best medics see a patient as an individual, but they don't live with your child day in, day out. They don't know the inner workings of your child's brain or see the incidents that worry and scare them (or you), which is why you are such an important part of the puzzle when it comes to care. You're a participant because you're affected by your child's illness, a spectator who can document what happens when and how, and a concerned party with your child's best interests at heart.

And this is why the best possible care programme is one that is a partnership between you, the parent/s, your child and the care team taking care of your child. Your child has a right to privacy, but if you can build strong relationships with your child's doctors, you will be removing one of the blocks to recovery and helping your child.

When you deal with hundreds of patients, I'm sure there's a drive to make the most impact and, in some cases, that can lead to a generalised approach: a reduction of broad and varied symptoms into a diagnosis that has a standardised initial treatment plan. And while we have to start somewhere and need to give things time to work, if you don't feel it's the right thing for your child, you have a voice and can express this.

DON'T BE AFRAID TO ASK TO SEE A DIFFERENT DOCTOR

I'm British and have been guilty of not asking for what I want in the past. But when my daughter became ill, I soon learned that if you don't ask, the answer is always no. Don't be afraid to ask to see another doctor or ask for a second opinion, if you think you need to.

Check reviews online and make friends with the receptionist. Ask them who they'd suggest seeing with a child with mental health issues. Listen for recommendations from friends and family. If you can't find a sympathetic doctor, consider moving practices to access the kind of considered care you're looking for.

DON'T BE AFRAID TO CHALLENGE

When I was told the waiting list for access to specialist care was months, I politely but firmly challenged our doctor to tell me what we were meant to do until that time. How were we meant to carry on in this state for week upon week until we got to the top of the list? He offered to see us weekly and, fortunately, it was at the next appointment that my daughter shared with him her intention to end her life, which led to her being seen by a psychiatrist the very next day. While not every situation will lead to this, it's important to be assertive, yet polite, and regularly visible.

If you're not being given options to access specialist care, mention to the doctor the kinds of treatments you're aware of (see page 242). Ask whether they think that would be a suitable option for your child and if they can be referred to your local mental health service. If the answer is no, ask for the referral criteria.

If you need to complain

If you don't get the kind of care you expect for your child, you do have routes to complain. It's always best to try to resolve these informally, not least for the benefit of your child. You can make a verbal complaint to the practice manager. With all complaints, a clear outline of what has happened and when will help to support your case and concerns. Keep notes on dates you saw professionals and what you were told. Build up a compelling, yet pragmatic picture of the shortcomings of the situation.

If you find yourself in the position where a formal complaint needs to be raised, there are prescribed routes for these, through the healthcare provider, the government or the General Medical Council in the UK.

The School Nurse/Counsellor

An alternative to speaking to your doctor if your child won't see them is to speak to the school nurse or counsellor. When my daughter was sliding into crisis, the school nurse gave us a safe space to come to terms with what was going on. There were many days where we both sat in her office, a box of tissues nearby, trying to make sense of what was happening.

School nurses can support your child in a number of ways. They can ensure that all teachers, the attendance officer and the school pastoral team are aware of your child's mental health issues. We'll speak about school on page 270, but, from a mental health perspective, the school nurse can generally offer more mental health support than teachers. School nurses can refer your child to the school counsellor, as well as arranging with the pastoral team for support in class. School nurses, as well as teachers, can refer to CAMHS, so if you can't get a referral from your GP, this is an alternative route.

Most schools now also have a school counsellor. Sadly generally oversubscribed, a school counsellor can also be a way to access some light-touch professional support without referral or waiting times and give your child someone outside of their daily life to share with. Despite school not always being the most therapeutic environment for children with a mental health issue, seeing the school counsellor gives children someone to explore their feelings with, and this can be a powerful and important step in them being heard. The school counsellor will work in confidence with your child, but should refer to more intense services if they feel it necessary.

Online Support

Giving your child some resources for them to explore without your input can be helpful too. Organisations like The Mix (themix.org.uk) offer wonderful support and advice for young people under 25 in the UK. They have a 1-2-1 chat plus a crisis messenger service, and heaps of information. There are similar services across the world – check the Parenting Mental Health website for localised support or see the Resources section (page 295) for some country-specific services.

Private Healthcare

We're not all in a financial position to access private healthcare, but if you do have it, check your policy and see if your child can be assessed by a private psychiatrist. They can diagnose and prescribe medication if appropriate and, if required, refer back to the NHS. This may be the fastest way to access psychiatric services and get a diagnosis and a treatment plan in place.

Charities offering support

If you can't access care through the NHS or it is taking too long, there are a number of charities that can help and offer counselling to your child, and the family too in some cases. There is more information about where to start in the Resources section on page 295.

Working With Mental Health Professionals

Your child may come into contact with a number of mental health professionals, from psychiatrists who can prescribe medication, to mental health nurses, psychologists, therapists and counsellors.

Generally, the first appointment with any professional will be an assessment to understand what your child is experiencing and any particular issues that may have contributed to the situation. With a psychiatric appointment, it is usually split to allow the professionals to get to know you and your child, both together and alone.

The psychiatrist will ask your child and you a number of questions. Some examples of the questions you and your child may be asked are:

- What has brought you here today?
- How long have you been feeling like this?
- How has your mood been recently?
- How are you finding school and your relationships with friends?
- What would you like to get from today's meeting?
- What kind of help would you prefer?
- Are you, or is anyone close to you, worried about your safety?

You and your child don't have to answer the questions they ask; however, the more information you can offer, the more likely and quicker it is that your child will get access to appropriate care. You will also have the chance to ask questions.

Your child may feel overwhelmed by the whole experience, so take some time before the appointment to discuss what is likely to happen and make it clear that they have the right to decline any questions and that this is an opportunity to share how they're really feeling to people who can help. This is the start of recovery if they can open up about how they're feeling.

If your child thinks they will struggle to share verbally, give them the opportunity to write down how they're feeling or to let you know what they want to be said. It's better if it comes from the child, but, with their permission, the professionals will certainly take on board what they have said through you.

> Opening yourself up to discuss your innermost thoughts, feelings and fears is a challenge for many of us. Doing it as a teenager, wondering what is right, wrong or downright strange, should be applauded. Be sure to tell your child that you respect them for taking these steps to get help, that you will support them throughout the process and that you will advocate for them if they want or need you to.

Before or after an appointment, you could reiterate to your teen that there may be things they don't want to share with you, and that that's OK. What they share with the psychiatric team will remain private unless the team has concerns for your child's safety or the safety of others. Before sharing anything with you as parents, the psychiatrist would always try to talk with your child about it first.

If you are a family with two parents, please try to both go along to the meeting. If you are a single parent, it is worth trying to bring along a close family friend or relative. Depending on what you are facing, you may need someone to support you, take notes or remind you afterwards of what was said. I spent many early appointments churning over a phrase or revelation, and then realised I was being asked a question I hadn't even heard. It's OK. But if you can have someone with you, it can really help.

If you have made notes on the changes you've seen in your child, take copies of these along to the assessment to leave with the team (see page 262). Try not to talk about your child as if they are not there. You're likely to get a chance to speak freely with the psychiatrist without your child and this is the time to share any concerns. You are the beacon of light in the dark sea of mental illness for your child. If you overshare in front of them, showing your own disappointment, fear or disdain for their behaviour or situation, you are likely to alienate them at a time when they are most in need of connection. Keep the focus on answering the psychiatric team's questions about your child factually, leaving out personal opinions, shame or blame.

At the end of the assessment, the team will let you know what the next steps are. They will write to you and other professionals involved, unless you have been referred due to crisis, when they are likely to be in touch by phone with next steps.

Issy was referred and seen immediately as she was at high risk of suicide. Our first meeting was a meeting of Aldersons and a clinical team of two, made up of a psychiatrist and a psychiatric nurse. Issy was prescribed medication on that day and a number of appointments were set up to start to unpick the why and how of her mental illness.

My husband and I were fully involved in this, having individual sessions with the psychiatrist to try to understand us as people, as parents and our family dynamic. I know that some people feel this is intrusive, almost like enforced therapy, but I really valued it. One of the by-products of this time was that Issy's psychiatrist helped me to understand my relationship with my father, and it helped me to heal as a person, enabling me to be a fully present, fully compassionate partner to my daughter throughout her illness. Don't be afraid of opening up. The teams aren't looking for reasons to blame you; in most cases, they won't find anything other than us being flawed human beings. In other cases, it can illuminate some of the reasons your child is in the situation they are in or the reason they remain stuck. Remember this is not a game of 'Blame the Parent'. It's a campaign to 'Help the Child'.

Speaking for your child

It can be easy when we're busy to speak for people. I see it with parents and children all the time. It's so important that everyone involved in caring for your child – you and your family, teachers, nurses, school counsellors, doctors, psychiatrists and psychologists – gives your child the space and time to express themselves. This is their illness, not ours. It is their experience and opinions that really craft the outcome of recovery. And whether it is marred by their illness or not, they have the right to a voice.

If you find yourself filling in the gaps with your child, ask yourself why. Is it because you're not sure if they've been clear? Are you concerned they don't know exactly what they feel? What they want to say? Or is it because you've been privy to other information that they are holding back?

Most professionals want to hear from the child themselves; after all, it is their illness. But what if your child can't articulate how they feel? What can you do when you have to be their literal voice, as well as their emotional advocate?

Initially, it's important to give your child the opportunity to speak or to at least try. Sometimes they think they can, and then they can't. Other times, they think they can't, yet the words spill out and they are able to articulate how they feel or, more likely, how they *don't* feel.

If you think it is likely that your child will not speak, ask them *before* the appointment if they would like you to speak on their behalf and be their voice. If they would, explain gently that you will be using their words and you won't be filling in the gaps. You are there to advocate for them, not to share your views, unless specifically requested. You could suggest asking them to write down their thoughts and share these directly with the professionals, or you could write down their thoughts if they prefer. This gives them the control of their care.

Sometimes it's important for the professionals to understand that you are speaking on their behalf, because it is their choice rather than your dominance. Opening up to someone you hardly know is challenging for most people, let alone those with a mental illness. Be clear with the doctor that you and your child have discussed what has been happening and have agreed that you will speak on their behalf to ensure everything is covered.

Remember that the clearer we are, the better the communication. It pays to be specific, and if your child can't be specific, offer them some suggestions but don't force them to choose.

> Your role is to try to shine a light on how they are feeling, not to offer a complete picture based on how you think you'd feel if you were in that situation.

Don't be tempted to speak about your child as if they weren't in the room. They are there, and they can hear you. Be compassionate and don't overlay your frustrations on the conversation, with comments such as, 'He is struggling to go to school and that's such a worry for me, because I have to work.' The professionals' primary interest is your child, not you. And your child hearing that you're under pressure because of their actions will do nothing for their peace of mind. The self-loathing, frustration and pointlessness of mental illness will be exacerbated by this. Remember your role: partnering your child through this time is to understand how they feel, rather than getting them to understand how you feel.

The professionals' approach

The focus of the professionals is on resilient recovery. They really want your child to not have to keep coming back! They want to return them to positive mental health. Some of the professional beliefs jarred with ours as parents. For example, most professionals working with children believe that school is the best place for young people with mental health issues – for routine, to reduce isolation and to maintain continuity. It all sounds eminently sensible, but if your child has a fear of school, has been bullied or attacked, or is put under pressure to achieve beyond their capacity, this belief can set them back and put you at odds with the professionals when you really need to be on the same page.

> ### Say thank you if you want to!
>
> Your GP and psychiatrist are doing a job and it's a hard one. Just as you live with mental illness every day, so do they. Thank them when they do a good job. Drop in some biscuits for the office if they've helped.

What if you don't think it's going to work?

If you have a feeling that something isn't going to work for your child, don't be afraid to speak up. Yes, they have experience of a multitude of mental disorders, but you know your child. Question yourself in a quiet moment. Is the feeling there because you never expected to be here and that's why agreeing to medication or interventions feels wrong? Or is it because you intuitively know that the suggested method will not be to your child's benefit? It's a fine line and, when we're in the midst of the chaos the initial diagnosis and engagement with professionals brings, it's easy to get swept along with agreeing to everything or nothing as you get your bearings on what you're facing.

Listening to your intuition is a key part of partnering your child through this time, and being open to the support professionals can offer is essential, as are the feedback and reactions of your child to what is being proposed. Sometimes you find a rhythm that suits you and your family; as long as it is not destructive, and if it can bring some calm and connection to an otherwise fraught and challenging time, cut yourself some slack.

Getting the most from your medical team

To recap, here's a list of how to approach dealing with your child's medical team:

- Keep your eyes on the prize – this is not about befriending anyone, it's not about proving you're a perfect parent or not a terrible one. It's about getting your child access to the treatment or support that they need.
- They are the professionals – respect that and their expertise. But they also don't know it all! You're bringing something important to the interaction too: knowledge and insight only you can know because you live with your child 24/7. They don't have a diploma in 'your kid'.
- It's your child – you know them best. Hold that thought. It's very important.
- Be confident. Be assertive where appropriate. Always, always be polite. The doctor and psychiatrist are people too. Respect works both ways. You're on the same side – it may not feel like it, but you are. You both want the same thing.
- Your child is mentally ill and may say things that are false. He or she may not want to share the realities of their life – this is not your fault.
- Your child is mentally ill and may hear things differently to how they were intended. Don't blow up over the facts, but do insist on collaboration to keep your child's treatment going.

- Be prepared – take your notes, write down your concerns, keep records. Don't be afraid to call and speak to the manager, the psychiatrist, or whoever you need to speak to, to get things done.
- If you feel you're not being heard, write an email explaining this and what you think needs to be taken on board. Try to extract your 'need to be heard' from what is helpful to your child's progress and treatment.
- Don't give up. Push on, with a smile.

The Language of Labelling and Diagnosis

To make sense of the nonsensical, we often rely on recognised terminology to bring order to a situation and help ourselves and others understand. A diagnosis is important to ensure the correct course of treatment is prescribed and followed and the structures of society can understand why your child can't engage with the 'norm'. A diagnosis can feel like a door opening to some, and like a prison to others.

Getting a diagnosis can reassure us and our child that they're not 'making it up'. It helps access specialist medical care, non-medical support in education, and can give access to financial support through state or charitable channels.

Pinning your hopes on to a diagnosis is understandable, because you want answers and to understand changes you may have seen in your child. But it's a fine line when it comes to the over-diagnosis of disorders. Other things need to be identified so they can be treated. And what your child feels is valid, with or without a medical term.

> Your child is your child before, during and after their diagnosis. Some things don't have to be explained, they can just be felt.

The challenge of a diagnosis can be that we now 'label' our child and look for behaviours and symptoms that are expected or anticipated. It can be used as a reason to stand down from boundaries and respect. And it can change how we subconsciously process hope and belief, leaving us feeling that our power to effect change is somehow lessened. That's simply not the case.

Partnering our child through mental illness means we stand alongside them as a person and are led by their needs, not their diagnosis. While we may seek out all available information as we serve our need for wisdom around something we don't have experience of, we understand that we can't apply a generalised diagnosis to a unique human being. We don't all fit in neat boxes. Diagnoses are helpful, but not prescriptive.

'You are not your diagnosis' was something we told Issy a lot. Fortunately, she was supported by a psychiatrist who believed in her ability to make a full recovery. The faith she placed in our daughter's bright, brilliant future enabled us all to see that there could be an end to this. It helped us to see the diagnosis of chronic depressive disorder and generalised anxiety disorder as things separate to her. We were responding to her, not treating a list of symptoms.

Whatever your child's diagnosis is, it isn't the end of the line. The diagnosis does not come with a judgement on your parenting skills. It does not determine their future or condemn them to a half-lived life. They won't need to declare it at customs. It does not define them, and it shouldn't stop them, or you, from living a life of note.

Dealing With School

School is often a word that strikes fear into children with a mental illness and their family. I could write a book just on this subject. The challenge with school is that everyone's experience is different, not least because every child and every school is different too.

Some schools are highly enlightened, with a well-being process and approach that recognises that the school environment doesn't suit everyone. Others can feel like the draconian equivalent of a Victorian workhouse, pumping out results at any price and ignoring the requirements that we all have: to be seen as an individual, to be heard and to have a level of autonomy over our actions.

The first thing to say about school is that it really doesn't matter. I am not decrying the formal education system completely; I am simply saying that when your child has a mental health issue, it is not the most important thing. It's not an indicator of their future worth as a person. The most important thing is their mental health.

There are examples in the Parenting Mental Health community where children have been able to function through school; every child will have their own experience. But if your child's mental health is interrupting their education or if they can't physically access school because of their mental illness, what do you do?

Talk to the school

If you're seeing the impact of school on your child's mental health and they're starting to ask to stay at home, it's time to have a chat with school. Your child might not want you to, but do it quietly and privately. The sooner the situation is communicated to school, the quicker they can make adjustments to support your child.

Approach your child's form teacher, head of year, pastoral support or the school nurse, and explain what is happening. If you can identify things that are increasing their anxiety or impacting on their mental health, highlight these and ask them for their suggestions on how the school can support them. If your child can't pinpoint what is making them feel depressed or anxious (or another mental disorder), explain that to the school.

Try not to show any exasperation or frustration at what is happening. If you can start to discuss your child's mental health in a pragmatic way, where it is a condition and not an annoyance, in the same way you would if your child had diabetes or a broken leg, it will help everyone. Your child won't feel like a 'burden', the school will know how you expect it to be spoken about and, by being clear about what is expected, you should hopefully get the kind of support and compassion that can make such a difference.

For example, maybe PE is an issue for your child. Suggest some workarounds: perhaps suggest you'd like them to sit this out for a few weeks to see if it has an impact on their mood towards school generally. Or if it's homework that is becoming an issue, explain you'd like to reduce the amount of homework and see if that helps.

Many schools have experience of children with mental health issues and will have some strategies in place. For example, schools can provide coloured cards that allow children to leave the classroom without notice. They can give them somewhere to go when they're struggling. They can allow them to not go to a particular class, form time or break, or wherever they are most anxious.

Check on the school's website for their SEND (special educational needs and disability) or mental health policy. According to a UK government paper published in 2018, 91 per cent of secondary schools have a SEND policy and 2 per cent have a mental health policy.

Make sure your child has a story ready to tell their friends, if they don't want to mention their mental health at this point.

If you haven't already, engage with the school nurse, who can offer access to the school counsellor and also refer to other services (see page 260).

You might feel like what's going on isn't bad enough to tell the school. If the tension that is generated is filtering across the family, it might be time. Maybe you're seeing the number of times your child is laughing and happy reduce. Maybe you're dreading Sunday nights as much as they are. Contact your child's form teacher or head of year and talk to them. However small and insignificant you fear others may view this as, the impact on your child and your family deserves attention. And it may help stop the decline of their mental health to something more serious.

If your child doesn't want to go to school

If your child's mental health continues to decline, you may find they are unable to attend school and you may be dealing with regular or sustained absences. Forcing your child to go to school when their mind is racing and debilitating their actions is not likely to end well. Not being able to do what you think they should can leave a child wondering what is wrong with them, and they can feel they are disappointing you, leading to them becoming isolated from the very person they should be able to lean on for support. If you can make it 'OK to not be OK', you'll find they won't be making excuses about school when they could be using that energy and space to start to make some kind of sense of what is going on in their heads and open up to you about it. There's always time for education and learning.

Here are some steps to take:

- Speak to your child and try to gently find out what is impacting on them, without judgement.
- Speak to school and explain what is going on.

- Follow up every interaction with the school with an email detailing what was said by whom and the next steps discussed and agreed.
- Don't be afraid to ask for special dispensations (see page 272).
- Speak about your child's situation with the pragmatism of any physical illness.
- Don't take no for an answer. Mental health is important and schools have to support their pupils. Check their policies on the school website (see page 272).

One of the parents in the Parenting Mental Health community shared that her son was studying for his GCSEs. He couldn't leave the house due to extreme anxiety, but the school expected him to somehow be able to get into school to take the exams. When it became apparent that he was not going to be able to do this, the family were told that he could not sit them at all, thereby penalising him for his poor mental health. I reviewed the school's SEND policy, and the arrangements exam boards put in place for children who are unable to sit exams in school, and we built a plan for the family. He was allowed to have home invigilation so he could complete his education.

A fresh start

As your child recovers, whether they've been in education throughout their illness or not, it may be that a fresh start is the best way to approach the next phase of their life. Mental illness offered my daughter an opportunity to get involved in a discipline she loved, at a younger age than had she continued her very academic education. Issy was at a school where academic results received the highest praise and it was hard to be valued for things that couldn't be graded. The things that made her brain and soul light up – creativity in all its forms, from thinking to drawing, sewing and gaming – were not measured by the school, and the kinds of career and learning paths they worked towards weren't really ever going to allow her to be her truest and best self.

I can say all this with the benefit of hindsight. While she was at the school, I believed I was doing the very best by sending her there. But mental illness changed everything, and I stepped down and stood beside her, so I could travel with her on the journey to recovery. This included letting go of what I thought she should do and stopping my hankering for the past so I could look towards a future for Issy designed by her.

After two years out of school, Issy was showing signs of progress. When a friend of mine mentioned a local college that specialised in digital arts, Issy said she would like to attend the open day. After that visit, any last thoughts we had as parents about her going back into the same education system ceased. To see her face light up at the prospect of learning about ideas and concepts that she was already exploring through her own curiosity was priceless. I couldn't quite believe it, but it was the beginning of two years of growth, driven by her and in a field that we would have never considered before mental illness.

Showing Issy that there were different opportunities available to her was instrumental in helping her to build upon her recovery and start to believe in the possibilities beyond the life and education we had all known. We encouraged her to be curious, which took the pressure off and introduced some joy and purpose into her life at a time where there was little.

Encouraging curiosity in our children is a more potent and empowering approach than demanding they do something that they find physically and emotionally challenging.

There are a number of ways that your child can and should be supported to engage in their education. From free online learning to vocational courses at colleges or traditional academic pathways, mental illness can be the starting point for a rich love of knowledge and growth. Encourage your child's curiosity, whether it's around baking, woodwork, music or game design. They are learning so much more than a curriculum when they are curious.

Don't give up

I know how wearing it is when you're battling: battling to understand what on earth has gone on with your child and where the funny, sweet person you know them to be has vanished to. Battling to juggle the expectations of school and family and work and medical appointments and life. But your child needs you to fight and to not give up. Taking a diversion due to mental illness doesn't mean your child will fail or isn't capable of learning in the future. I am constantly delighted by stories of parents who have challenged schools on their rules and fought to access the right approach for their child. Remember the power you have as a parent to effect change – to challenge where necessary and to represent your child's needs.

Keep in mind . . .

1. Healthcare professionals and parents share the same goal – to help a child recover and thrive. You can work together to achieve that goal.

2. Education takes many forms and there are many ways to access it throughout your child's life. School may work for some and not for others. Many schools will be able to help you if you start the dialogue with them.

3. Remember that you know your child best, so don't be afraid to challenge school or professionals to get them the support they need.

14

The Worst Days

The worst day is a portent of change, whether you like it or not, and, strange as it may sound, it can actually be the best day for you and your child.

I guess you've turned to this chapter because you or your child (probably both) are having a really bad day. Perhaps the worst day you have had so far. Maybe every day feels like your child's worst day, to you and to them. Fighting a mental illness is debilitating and overwhelming, and, even on the days where we feel there is progress, life delivers another challenge or issue and the fragments of resilience we have been nurturing are shattered. Or you may be reading this to help you look back and reflect on the day you realised that your child had descended into crisis, so you can find some hope in the details.

Mental illness makes itself known in quiet ways at first. It gently taps you on the shoulder and, if you don't acknowledge it, it starts to scream and demand immediate attention. We become very adept at ignoring this noise and justifying it away. What is happening won't stop because you don't accept it or it doesn't fit in with your expectations of life. Confronting the 'worst day' and the circumstances that have led to it affords you an opportunity to do everything in your power to define the outcomes. The decision to heed its call takes courage. It can herald a new start as well as an end to what you've known so far.

A Child's Worst Day

You may feel like you know what your child's worst day is. It may surprise you that it isn't the day they attempt to end their life or get so anxious in school that they have a panic attack in class. Your child's worst day might be the one where they decide they don't believe in their potential for recovery. It might be the day they watch you sob silently through the gap in the bathroom door and feel even worse for feeling they've brought this enemy into your hearts and home. It might be the day they find themselves exhausted from trying to push themselves forward and fail. Or the day they are shown for certain they have no control over their life.

Young people don't tell us everything. A mix of fear of judgement, fear of misunderstanding and of not wanting to hurt or disappoint us can mean they hold on to emotions that damage them deeply and would be eased if they shared. It can be with the purest of intent to shield us from their pain or because they don't believe we will understand or empathise. Let's hear from Issy about what it was like on her worst day:

'On my worst day, I went in to school late on purpose to avoid people and the possibility of having to speak to them. I couldn't cope with what they might say and I hated being alone in the form room. The teachers didn't always support me and I sometimes felt that they were actually part of the bullying. I realised that they're not the impartial authority figures you want them to be. You want to be able to go to them, but very often I felt like a nuisance and I couldn't get the support I needed. My games teacher (who was my form teacher too) let me go and sit quietly in the library. Thinking back it was probably to make her life easier, but I don't mind that. It made mine easier too.

I was called out for not knowing an answer by one teacher before lunch and I could feel my heart rate increase and my face go red. I couldn't cope with all the faces looking at me and the judgements I saw in their eyes. At lunch I walked aimlessly around, with no friends to speak to and nowhere to go. I was just trying to fight through to get home. In the last lesson of the day, which was normally a calm space for me, a girl threw a book at me. She said sorry sarcastically, and I said, "That's OK", trying to make the situation easier and shut it down. And then she laughed at my voice, imitated me in front of the whole class and said something about me being weak. Everyone seemed to laugh and at that point I thought, I've done everything right and yet I'm still getting shit thrown at me. I can't win at this. I have nowhere to go.

I got home and went to bed. I had no friends, so no one texted me. I scrolled through social media and that just made me feel more isolated and demoralised. I lay there thinking what is the point? I was desperate. There was no way out. I couldn't stop this or change it. This was the worst day because I knew then what I had to do. I had no choice. I had to kill myself.'

This powerful account gives us an insight into the circumstances and emotions that led Issy to decide to end her life. As an adult, you can see how you might respond differently to this situation and how you might deal with it. You could take yourself out of the situation. You could reflect on the fact you are doing nothing wrong, and that it is the bully with the problem, and not your fault. But as you can see from the words above, a child can't always do that.

When someone has been traumatised, marginalised or bullied, had belief in their ability to effect change challenged, and had their mental balance and emotional peace taken away, often in sight of people in authority who have overlooked the facts and the impact, it is deeply sad and yet understandable that mental health issues arise. In some cases, thoughts of suicide appear to be the only option, the only choice they have control of. The loss of power and agency over their life turns a multicoloured future full of potential into a monochrome moment when nothing holds any hope and their only chance of control comes from the choice over whether they live or die.

When you have no power and you feel the world is conspiring to keep it that way, it's completely understandable why people feel this is their only alternative. I think society can try to distil young people's very deep, very real feelings into simplistic terms. They're not 'just' teenagers putting us through the mill; they're not just going through 'hormonal changes'. They're not 'snowflakes' or attention seekers.

> Children are 'connection seekers', desperate to find their place and people, and to make sense of a world that is erratic and unfair.

How to talk on the worst day

Keeping the lines of communication open is key. We can't assume we know or understand what our child is going through; we're not in their heads and our experience is not theirs. Our recollections of our adolescence are personal and different.

Be a safe space for them. Assume positive intent when they share. Allow them to say what they feel and to feel OK about feeling it. Open up about your own experiences if you've struggled with your mental health, if you think it will help with communication; it's something we all wrestle with to a greater or lesser extent.

Don't make assumptions or gloss over the difficult parts. Sitting on the kitchen floor late into the night listening to Issy tell me why she wanted to end her life and begging me to let her do it was some of the worst emotional pain I have ever encountered. My goal was to keep her alive, but shutting off her reasons behind it because I didn't want them to be true would have invalidated her in the ultimate moment of vulnerability.

Resist making assumptions about how your child should respond to certain situations. What they feel and do might not chime with you, but forget yourself for a moment and consider why they are in crisis. What pain are they escaping from? What control are they trying to take?

And if that all feels like you're indulging them, put down your fear and let go of any judgement for a moment and see them for what they are: a scared, isolated person in need of love, understanding and connection. Your child. In need of your support, belief and acceptance. Give them what they need, without question.

> If at any stage you feel you cannot keep your child safe, do not hesitate to take them to A&E or to call 999.

A Parent's Worst Day

Your worst day can come at any point in this experience of helping a child with a mental health illness. It might be for a completely different reason to your child's and it might not need a specific trigger to happen. Sometimes, a word, a feeling, a song even, completes a circuit in our mind and we find ourselves dealing with a rush of emotion that seems to come from nowhere. The processing of heightened emotions and unmet expectations, and the release of long-held hopes and dreams, is going on all the time in our subconscious brain, and it's normal for us to come to a point where we have to let these out.

You may feel you've been managing your child's mental health for some time and that you've dodged the obstacles so far. And then you'll get a call from school or the parent of one of their friends telling you about extreme behaviour, self-harm or a suicide plan. Something might bring into sharp focus the reality that your skills, influence and experience are not working, and may even be harming your child and building a barrier between the two of you.

You might find yourself going from a picture of serenity to a wild banshee in a nanosecond, telling your child a whole load of unnecessary truths about their behaviour and demonstrating the kind of emotion that you try to rein in when they display it.

You might have to confront the harsh evidence of your child's self-harm or suicide attempts; seeing their perfect form cut, burned or hooked up in a hospital bed, their face devoid of hope and belief, empties your heart. You can't imagine life being worse than this moment.

A worst day might come along when you least expect it. Your child might be stable, improving or moving forward and then you find yourself unable to stop crying, unable to control the flood of emotions that you were convinced you had under wraps. It might be the day you return their sports equipment or send their school books back and you feel something has definitely ended. It might be the day your body feels like lead and won't let you move from bed.

What can you do on your worst day?

None of this is easy. I understand; I have lived it too. When I was pregnant with Issy, my son asked me if I'd have enough love for both of them when she arrived. Put on the spot, I told him a story that each baby comes with its own special delivery of love so there was plenty to go around. I made this up in the moment as a way to calm his worry, but I think it works for us as parents too. When we become a parent, we're given strength and love. In the moments when you feel you don't have the power to access strength and love, please know you have something special inside yourself. It is mighty and it is powerful. You really do have the strength to get your family through this.

- Remind yourself, or set now, your core family goal (see page 178). This might be simply to get through this, to help your child get well.
- Today, prioritise yourself. Turn down the noise of life and buy yourself some space to deal with the flashes that challenge your life every day.
- Give yourself the grace and space to recognise and process everything you are going through.

SELF-CARE

When your child is in crisis, the last thing on your mind is self-care; it may feel flippant and pointless, but now is the most important time for self-care, even if you feel you may not be able to face it. We need nurture and strength more than ever and the worst day is an unexpected invitation to introduce more self-care to your life (see Chapter 9).

The worst day can be a catalyst for a dive into negative 'self-care', where we inhale sugar or alcohol or overspend. Sometimes that's the only way we feel we can get through and that's OK. But we can't stay there for long, for everyone's sake.

Give the worst day the respect it deserves because, if we're not careful, it can become the worst week, or month, or year. If the worst-day behaviour persists, listen up. It's telling you something about yourself and you absolutely must listen, for everyone's sake.

It's OK to ask for help

If the worst day is becoming every day and you don't know how you will continue to cope, call your doctor. Book to see a counsellor. Make that appointment. Get some support. There is absolutely no shame in asking for help. Being the blueprint for your child doesn't mean never falling down, but it does mean always getting up, somehow.

Compassion Fatigue

So many of us hold on so tightly to what we think we can control to counter the uncertainty of our child's illness, we can overlook the impact of being a long-term carer. We find ourselves forced into patterns of behaviour that we didn't choose. We ask ourselves and our children questions that none of us can possibly answer: Why you? Why us? When will this be over? What did I do to create this? The impact of this situation needs to be recognised and addressed at some point, and you might find the cracks beginning to show as your family finds itself coming through the darkest days.

What is compassion fatigue?

Tanja Sharpe, a counsellor and coach, describes a very real condition that affects a lot of us who care for someone over the long term:

'Compassion fatigue and exhaustion in parents who support a child through mental illness is now affecting more parents than ever before. The symptoms can be severe and are likened to post-traumatic stress disorder (PTSD) as a result of surviving on the battlefield. The difference for these parents is that the battlefield is in their home daily, and they are often trying desperately to keep their most loved ones alive and well. It is constant stress, worry and fight or flight that can cause long-term chronic stress, fatigue and burnout.

'As a counsellor I am seeing many more parents who are now experiencing the symptoms of compassion fatigue as well as dealing with burnout and unexplained illnesses in the body that have similar symptoms to chronic stress. I have noticed that common physical symptoms and behaviours can link to certain patterns of thinking, including:

- Exhaustion. A feeling that 'I have nothing left to give.'
- Inability to listen to others and show compassion: 'My well is empty and I simply can't hear anymore.'
- Earaches. This could be a result of 'turning off from the world'.
- Headaches. This could be: 'I'm overwhelmed by worrying thoughts.'
- Low moods or mood swings, linked with struggling to find balance.
- Irritability. An expression of: 'Can't you see I have bigger problems?!'
- Sore muscles and body pains from stress and often lactic acid in the muscles. A physical manifestation of 'I am so tense.'

- Skin rashes: 'I feel so irritated with the world and my situation.'
- Dry mouth: 'I can't speak anymore' or 'I can't find the words to speak.'
- Nausea and stomach pains could be tension or 'I'm worrying so much.'
- Painful periods: 'I don't feel safe for me or for my child.'
- Sore joints: 'I'm afraid and I don't know how to move forward.'
- Sleep disturbance or wanting to sleep all the time: 'I don't know what to do, this is too hard.'
- Loss of intimacy or pleasure: 'I'm exhausted and I don't have the right to experience pleasure.'
- Emotional numbness: 'I don't want to feel anymore.'
- Crying or weepiness: 'I just want to let it out.'
- Eye strain or blurriness: 'I can't see my way forward, I'm exhausted.'
- Painful feet, legs or any part of your body that you associate with moving forward in life: 'I can't see a future.'
- Loss of appetite: 'I can't eat because what's the point?'
- Cravings: 'A quick fix to make me feel better, give me more energy to cope.'
- Increased blood pressure: 'I'm so stressed out.'
- Lower immunity from illness: 'I can't be well if he/she isn't well.'
- Colds and flu (often only lasting a day): 'I need to rest.'

'Our bodies are in what I call "chemical chaos", when we are experiencing these levels of stress and fatigue and the body is constantly in fight or flight mode. It can take anything from 30 minutes to a few days to return to a normal state of relaxation and balance, but, as parents who face these situations daily, we often don't have the opportunity to rest and balance the body.'

Looking back on my own worst days

For all of the positivity I feel about the experience we had, there is no denying that it was a long and painful one. I definitely ticked off a lot of the symptoms on Tanja's list above. Yes, this experience changed us all for the better, and I wouldn't change what we've been through, but that change took its toll. There were some days where I wondered if my heart was physically capable of holding any more hurt. Most days, I felt the emotional pain in a very physical way and it was only when I quietly decided that this was not the way our story was going to end that I began to take some control and believe in the possibility of a new 'new normal' on our terms.

Going Forward For You

Embracing the fallout from the worst day can be as simple as saying that you need a new set of skills to help change things. It can be a commitment to doing something different, because you know you can't carry on as you are. It can be a quiet admission to yourself that change has to come from you.

If I had had the confidence and awareness to have gone all-in with partnering when Issy first showed the signs of poor mental health 18 months before she was in crisis, I am unsure if I would be here writing this. If I had had the presence of mind to challenge the 'common sense' that told me to send her to school, and instead had shielded her sooner, who knows what would have happened? Maybe she wouldn't have become ill.

We have a choice as parents. We can choose to continue, following the rules of life that we're bombarded with, following the ways we're told to live and love, or we can be brave and prioritise wholeheartedly our commitment to our family's happiness and needs. This means huge amounts of self-reflection, painful change, new skills and a bravery that most of us don't believe we have, when really we do.

Keep in mind . . .

1. Your child's worst day might come out of the blue or there may have been signs. You might not understand exactly why, but you must pay attention. There is help out there if you need it – do take it.
2. You need to look after yourself during your worst days. You are important and valuable, and hold the key to how your family responds to this experience.
3. The worst days can be the days when we learn the most: what we need to change, what we need to action and how we move forward. Don't be afraid to take these learnings on board.

Epilogue

Never Let Go

The impacts of mental illness on families run deep. If you've lived through any kind of mental health issue, you'll understand that the desperation, isolation, dread and fear that permeate the everyday aren't easy to overlook or overcome. Society is still learning how to deal effectively with mental illness and how to support families.

But for all of the isolation, you are not alone. And for all of the bleakness, there is hope. I held on to hope throughout Issy's illness, even when I had no idea how I could or why I should.

I've seen things that no parent should see. I imagine you feel like that too. I've wept more tears that I thought possible and my head has almost exploded many times from the weight of worry I've carried. But, somehow, hope reminded me that we were on a journey of discovery and, if we could make it through, it would be the making of us all.

Partnering Issy through her illness has been a transformative experience for all of us. It opened us up to the truest parts of ourselves and enabled us to create the strongest bond. I cherish deeply the connection I have with her; it is beyond anything I could have imagined before she got ill. It has been an absolute privilege to care for her through mental illness and it is something I would not go back and change. It has been a life-affirming experience to face my fears – my past, her present, our future – and decide that we were going to beat this, on our terms.

Maintaining a relationship with your child is a lifelong pursuit. Yes, there may be a very urgent need that is driving your behaviour: the need to keep your child alive. But even in the gravest of times, looking to the future and to our bigger purpose as a parent helps us to make better decisions. Not only are we trying to keep a child alive, we are trying to build a mutual respect and relationship beyond their adolescence.

And if that isn't a big enough goal, we are actually looking ahead to our children's children and how we make an impact on them. By changing the behaviour that you display in your home and by changing the way that you speak to your child and see your relationship with them, you are laying the foundations for a whole new generation of parenting through your child. If your child becomes a parent, they'll look to how they were treated as a blueprint for their behaviour. They'll have a different set of behavioural tools to parent/partner their children. If they ever find themselves in the devastating situation that you find yourself in, they'll instinctively know how to respond, thanks to you.

For us as parents, despite being counter-intuitive, partnering offers a release of expectation, pressure to conform and pressure to fix. Partnering teaches patience, with yourself, your child and with change. It helps guard you against an impatient world that expects linear progress and judges anything but.

Most of all, partnering gifts you a power at a time when you possibly feel the most powerless you have ever felt. This power is not to control or demand, but to accept, to nurture and to build the strongest connection possible with your child.

The ripple effects of partnering your child reach far and wide, beyond your child and beyond your home. You get a sense of what's really important and make deep connections that really matter. For example, you may now approach relationships with a sense of not having to control, of not having to have all the answers. That can make relationships less fraught and more meaningful. Powerful understanding, compassion and connection bloom from the darkness of the challenge you face. You find that you have not been buried, as you may have thought. You have been planted.

It may seem strange and somewhat outlandish to 'thank' mental illness for its impact on our lives. I don't want anyone to suffer the distress and chaos it brings, but the opportunity it gave me to understand what love really looks like is priceless. I hope that at some point you are able to look back at this time and cherish the changes you have made and the connection you have forged with your child.

Seeing this as an opportunity to understand yourself better is a positive by-product of this time. You may feel overwhelmed and consumed by fighting your child's mental illness, but, under the bonnet, there's plenty of change happening in you too. This experience can make you better or bitter, and the choice is all yours. Start the day with the expectation that your interactions will teach and enrich you, and yes, there may be some challenge, but you will find that a sense of peace will gradually grow inside you

Caring for someone with compassion challenges us and what we believe we know about ourselves. It insists we reflect on how we communicate, what our expectations and assumptions are, and how present we are as a parent. But it opens up an opportunity to be human. And to create a lifelong connection, as people, not just parents. This experience has shown me the true power we hold in our hands as parents, to gently influence, nurture and care for the burgeoning young people we've been privileged to raise. To be kind to them in their time of need. And to be kind to ourselves in ours.

Lifting up the next generation, particularly when society and its structures can't, is work we parents must do. And for the challenges this and coming generations face, partnering is an antidote to disconnection. We can create meaningful change in our homes with the simplest of tools, available to us all, whatever our backgrounds – acceptance, patience, trust, love and respect. We can shield our children from the judgement and fear, so they can heal for the long term. And we can build a resilient generation, of the most compassionate young people, who have faced more than they should at their tender age, but who now see the world through different eyes.

I hope the next generation of young people will grow up knowing their mental health is as important as their physical health. I hope that they feel complete whatever their mental state, and that there is a place for them in a world that is prepared to do what is necessary to reduce the numbers of young people with mental illness. I take great hope from the many 'success stories' from parents I speak to in the Parenting Mental Health community, where they share how they have dealt with mental illness and now see their child flourishing, despite all they have faced.

Please know that you are doing important and valuable work. You aren't *just* a parent; you are an advocate, a change-maker and a beacon of hope for your child, yourself and your family. Shine bright for everyone who has had to deal with mental illness, even when you're tired and worn out.

We all have the ability and the power to change our story. You can decide today that this is not the way your family's story will end.

Be brave, be kind and, please, never let go of hope.

Resources

To find out more about **Parenting Mental Health,** join the PMH support group: www.facebook.com/parentingmentalhealth

To find out more about the programmes and training we run, and to access the resources mentioned throughout the book, visit: www.parentingmentalhealth.com/book

Information on Treatments

BrainWorking recursive therapy (BWRT)

The Terence Watts BWRT Institute
https://www.bwrt.org/

Cognitive behavioural therapy (CBT)

https://www.nhs.uk/conditions/cognitive-behavioural-therapy-cbt/

Counselling

The British Association for Counselling and Psychotherapy
https://www.bacp.co.uk/

Dialectical behaviour therapy (DBT)

https://www.mind.org.uk/information-support/drugs-and-treatments/dialectical-behaviour-therapy-dbt/about-dbt/

Eye movement desensitisation and reprocessing (EMDR)

EMDR UK
https://emdrassociation.org.uk/

Hypnotherapy

The National Hypnotherapy Society
https://www.nationalhypnotherapysociety.org/

Psychotherapy

UK Council for Psychotherapy
https://www.psychotherapy.org.uk/

Finding a Therapist

UK

The British Association for Counselling and Psychotherapy
https://www.bacp.co.uk/

USA

American Counseling Association
https://www.counseling.org/aca-community/learn-about-counseling/what-is-counseling/find-a-counselor

American Mental Health Counselors Association
https://www.amhca.org/home

American Psychological Association
https://locator.apa.org/

BetterHelp
https://www.betterhelp.com/online-counseling/

Australia

Australian Association of Family Therapy
https://www.aaft.asn.au/find-a-therapist/

Australian Psychological Society
https://www.psychology.org.au/Find-a-Psychologist

Psychotherapy and Counselling Federation of Australia
https://www.pacfa.org.au/find-a-therapist/

Support for Your Child

Global support

7 Cups
https://www.7cups.com/

UK

Crisis Messenger Service
Text SHOUT to 85258 in the UK to text with a trained Crisis Volunteer.

Kooth
https://www.kooth.com/

NHS Go
https://nhsgo.uk/

The Mix
https://www.themix.org.uk/

USA

American Foundation for Suicide Prevention
Call 800-273-8255 or 988 or text TALK to 741741

IMAlive
Visit https://www.imalive.org/online/ to access online chat

The Trevor Project (for LGBTQ youth)
Call 1-866-488-7386 or text START to 678678
Visit https://www.thetrevorproject.org/ to access online chat

Australia

Beyond Blue
Call 1300 22 4636
Visit https://www.beyondblue.org.au/ to access online chat

Headspace
Call the Suicide Call Back Service on 1300 659 467
Visit https://headspace.org.au/emergency-assistance/ to access online chat

Kids Helpline
Call 1800 55 1800
Visit https://www.kidshelpline.com.au/ to access the Lifeline Text service

Lifeline
Call 13 11 14
Visit https://www.lifeline.org.au/ to access the Lifeline Text service

Charities Offering Support

UK

Anxiety UK
https://www.anxietyuk.org.uk/get-help/

BEAT Eating Disorders
https://www.beateatingdisorders.org.uk/

Bullying UK
https://www.bullying.co.uk/

Hub of Hope
https://hubofhope.co.uk/

OCD UK
https://www.ocduk.org/

Nightline Association
A student listening service that is open at night and run by students for students
https://www.nightline.ac.uk/

No Panic
A registered charity that helps people who suffer from panic
attacks, phobias, obsessive compulsive disorders and other related
anxiety disorders as well as their carers
https://nopanic.org.uk/

Papyrus: Prevention of Young Suicide
https://papyrus-uk.org/

Relate
https://www.relate.org.uk/relationship-help/help-children-and-
young-people

Rethink Mental Illness
https://www.rethink.org/

Safeline
For everyone affected by or at risk of sexual abuse and rape
https://www.safeline.org.uk/

Samaritans
Call 116 123
Email jo@samaritans.org
https://www.samaritans.org/

stem4: Supporting Teenage Mental Health
https://stem4.org.uk/

Zero Suicide Alliance
https://www.zerosuicidealliance.com/
Take their free training: https://www.zerosuicidealliance.com/
training

USA

Active Minds
Supporting mental health awareness and education for young
adults
https://www.activeminds.org/

American Foundation for Suicide Prevention
https://afsp.org/

Child Mind Institute
https://childmind.org/

Mental Health America
https://mhanational.org/

National Alliance on Mental Illness
www.nami.org

National Institute of Mental Health (NIMH)
The lead federal agency for research on mental disorders
https://www.nimh.nih.gov/

Samaritans USA
http://www.samaritansusa.org/

Australia

Headspace
https://headspace.org.au/

Mental Health Australia
https://mhaustralia.org/

Book Contributors

Zanneta Neale
Chartered Psychologist, Chartered Scientist, Associate Fellow of
the British Psychological Society, Registered Coaching
Psychologist and Registered Occupational Psychologist with the
Health and Care Professions Council
zanneta@me.com

Tanja Sharpe
Qualified Integrative Counsellor MBACP
Professional Member of the British Association for Counselling
and Psychotherapy and
the American Association for Neuro-Linguistic Programming and
Hypnotherapy
www.tanjasharpe.com
www.creativecounsellorsassociation.org

Jane Hutton

Jane holds qualifications in nutritional therapy, clinical nutrition and food and environmental allergies, with further training and study in functional medicine and naturopathy. She holds a PGCE and is an approved practitioner of the Complementary Medical Association

https://www.functional-foodie.com/

http://www.trinityholistics.co.uk/

Acknowledgements

Thank you Issy. You allowed me into the darkness of your world when you were so poorly and scared, and trusted me with your difficult truths. You have graciously shared your experience, and that you were open to helping others when you were still hurting so much is testament to your character and compassion. We have grown so much. Thank you for bringing some of the moments of our experience to life with your beautiful illustrations.

Jack, thank you for being the kindest, happiest, most insightful and committed son and companion. Your vision and belief in what's possible help me be a better person. You and Issy will never know just what you and your support means to me.

Ross, you have seen me through the highs and lows of creating this book and of my life. You have shaped my thinking and filled in the gaps where I'd blocked out the darkest of times. I couldn't have done any of this without you.

Margaret Willson, thank you for showing me how to be a strong woman and never giving up on me or my children. Jim would be so proud, wouldn't he? To Elizabeth Flesher, thank you for showing me the power of hard work, tenacity and commitment. Your support means the world.

This book would not have happened without a team of talented people, including my agent, Sophie Bradshaw, who saw something in our story and helped to get it out of my head; thanks for your passion for this project and your pragmatism and belief. Thanks to the team at Penguin Random House, including Sam Jackson for commissioning the book and being

so patient with this first-timer. Thanks to the delightful Becky
Alexander whose calm and insightful approach shaped this
book and helped me learn so much. And to Julia Kellaway,
thank you for your kind, conscious and considerate efforts. I
am sad that this book resonated with you, but it is better for
your sensitivity and influence. Thank you to Zanne for your
contributions, and for a lifetime of the best friendship; to
Tanja, my non-collab collaborator, for your wisdom; and to
Jane for your knowledge and openness to help.

I may have founded the Parenting Mental Health (PMH)
community, but it has been built through the stories of
thousands of brave parents. To those who have shared,
contributed their experiences to the book or sent me support
along the way, thank you. You have kept me going.

To the PMH Admin Team past and present – Joy Walker,
Diane Angus, Joanne Shalliker, Karen Smythe and Sara
Simpson. Thank you for your commitment, support and
friendship. A special 'obrigado' to our angels, Susie Neves and
Ellie Shiel.

The following PMH Gratitudents stepped in to write the
Daily Gratitude, which helped me so much: Abi Fox, Alyshea
Techam, Andrea Westlake, Bryony Ridout, Caroline Rusack,
Corinne Austin-Sturgeon, Dawn Speechley, Dawn Thompson,
Denise Marsh, Elizabeth Schub Kamir, Isabelle Kinney, Jamie
Brimhall, Jane Quirk, Janet Robertson, Jennifer Corbett
Lones, Jenny Brown, Jill Walsh, Jo Harbord, Lois Gent, Lynne
Butterworth, Nicky Bristow, Pam May, Penny de la Mare,
Sarah Cooper, Sherry Hrozensky, Shona Honeyman, Shona
MacPherson, Teresa Hewitson and Tricia Greenwood. Thank
you.

To the friends who believed in me even more than usual:
Nikki Neale, Mel Bound of 'This Mum Runs', Alexandra
Davison of 'Live Life Well', Pippa Jamie, Mike and Dawn

Duck, Sue Flesher, Nikki Sparkes, Fiona Penhallurick, Susan Camm and my goddaughter, Caroline Camm.

The past few years have brought many extraordinary people into my life, including George Gabriel: 'If I am not for myself, who will be for me? If I am for myself alone, what am I? If not now, when?' What a gift you have been over the past two years. Thank you for seeing me and spurring me on to think bigger and push for greater impact. And Alex Hazan, thank you for always believing in and pushing me. Your insight and commitment has changed so much for me and PMH. Here's to fishing!

And finally, for playing such an important role in Issy's recovery, I deeply appreciate the commitment of Mr Smith at BOA who was such a positive mentor for Issy. Thanks also to Dr Ryan Prince, whose support calmed many difficult days, Donna Trim and Issy's NHS psychiatric team.

Index

A&E (Accident & Emergency) 15, 23, 43, 216, 283
acceptance 29, 59, 61, 74, 76, 77, 81, 83, 84, 85, 86, 99, 102–5, 106, 109, 110–11, 112, 115, 124, 130, 132, 141, 196, 201, 202, 210, 215, 232, 245, 283, 292, 294
  accepting the situation 104
  accepting you 104–5
  accepting your child 104
  defined 103
  finding it hard to accept 103
  move into 102–5
acknowledgement 12, 13, 30, 40, 51, 61, 69, 93–102, 115, 124, 141, 149, 220, 245, 279
  your behaviour and its impacts 97–9
  your child's mental health 95–7
  your power to affect change in your life 99–100
  your reality versus their reality 101–2
  your strengths and needs 100–1
adaptively, living 110
adversity, opportunities to evolve and 44–5
affirmations 170–1
alcohol 31, 57, 60, 285–6
Alderson, Issy ii, 19, 20, 22, 23, 29, 34, 35, 36, 37, 38, 39, 42, 43, 44, 70, 71, 72, 77, 166, 170, 196, 197, 215, 231, 238, 242, 244, 264, 270, 275, 285, 289, 291

bullying of 7–14, 22, 31, 140, 280–2
communication and 120, 124, 126, 127, 128, 133, 134, 138, 139, 140, 143, 146–7
partnering and 79, 80, 82, 83, 85, 86, 88, 89, 93, 94, 95, 102, 105, 107, 108, 111, 114
recovery from mental illness 4
slide into mental illness, memory of 30–2
story of mental illness 7–16
suicidal thoughts 8, 9–10, 14–15, 29, 34, 39, 42, 48, 49, 71, 114, 145, 197, 264
worst day 280–3
Alderson, Ross ii, 9, 10, 11, 12, 15, 23, 36, 44, 48, 50, 107, 218, 264
alienation 22–3, 136, 255
Angelou, Maya 51
anger 31, 34, 41, 42, 57, 58, 81, 97, 108, 113, 185, 201, 207, 230
anxiety 7, 11–12, 18, 37, 38, 40, 70, 76, 87, 113, 121, 182, 183, 209, 220, 223, 225, 255, 256, 270, 271–2, 274, 280
  cancer and 23
  CBD oil and 244
  eating and 227
  exercise/activity and 235
  gut health and 225, 226
  hypnotherapy and 245
  physical health and 22, 23
  rates of among teenagers 22, 23, 24
  sleep and 229, 230